ADVANCES IN STEREO VISION

Edited by **José R.A. Torreão**

Advances in Stereo Vision
Edited by José R.A. Torreão

Published by InTech
Janeza Trdine 9, 51000 Rijeka, Croatia

Publishing Process Manager Davor Vidic

Technical Editor Teodora Smiljanic

Cover Designer InTech Design Team

Additional hard copies can be obtained from orders@intechopen.com

Advances in Stereo Vision, Edited by José R.A. Torreão
p. cm.
ISBN 978-953-307-837-3

For EU product safety concerns:
IN TECH d.o.o., Prolaz Marije Krucifikse Kozulić 3, 51000 Rijeka, Croatia,
info@intechopen.com or visit our website at intechopen.com.

Meet the editor

José R.A. Torreão holds a B.Sc. and an M.Sc. in Physics from the Federal University of Pernambuco, Brazil, and an M.Sc. in Engineering and a Ph.D. in Physics from Brown University, USA. He has held appointments with the Federal University of Pernambuco and the Pontifical Catholic University of Paraná, and is currently a Professor with the Computing Institute of the Fluminense Federal University, in Niterói, Brazil, where he has acted for two terms as Head of the Graduate Program. His research interests are in computer and biological vision.

Contents

Preface

Stereopsis is a vision process whose geometrical foundation has been known for a long time, ever since the experiments by Wheatstone, in the 19th century. Nevertheless, its inner workings in biological organisms, as well as its emulation by computer systems, have proven elusive, and stereo vision remains a very active and challenging area of research nowadays. In this volume we have attempted to present a limited but relevant sample of the work being carried out in stereo vision by researchers from around the world. We have chapters dealing with the implementation of stereo algorithms in dedicated hardware; with active stereo vision systems; with stereo based on omnidirectional images; with the application of stereo vision to robotic manipulation and to environment modeling; with the psychophysical aspects of stereo, and with the interface between biological and artificial stereo systems. Thus, we believe that we have covered significant aspects of stereopsis, both from the applied and from the theoretical standpoints.

We would like to thank all the authors who contributed to this project, and also the editorial staff at InTech, especially Mr. Vidic, for their continuous support.

José R.A. Torreão
Instituto de Computação
Universidade Federal Fluminense
Brazil

1

Active Stereo Vision for 3D Profile Measurement

Jing Xu[1], Qiang Yi[1], Chenglong Fu[1], Huabin Yin[2], Zhengda Zhao[2] and Ken Chen[1]
[1]*Tsinghua University*
[2]*AVIC Chendu Aircraft Industrial(Group)Co., Ltd*
China

1. Introduction

Over the past decade, vision-based 3D sensing technology has been increasingly applied in manufacturing industries. The 3D shape of a part, which can be represented by using a point cloud, is usually required for two main purposes: reverse engineering or dimensional inspection. On the other hand, vision-based 3D sensing techniques can be divided into categories: passive stereo vision and active stereo vision.

Stereo vision based on no additional devices besides the cameras is known as passive stereo vision, which works in a similar way as the human eyes. In this case, the passive stereo vision can be very compact and low-cost without any extra components. The extensive application of the passive vision benefits from the epipolar geometry, first introduced in (Longuet, 1981). Epipolar geometry, which provides the geometric constraints between 2D image points in the two cameras relative to the same 3D points with the assumption that the cameras can be presented by using the pinhole model, has been utilized in camera calibration. However, it still has some drawbacks for industrial inspection. The first difficulty is the correspondence problem. In other words, determining the pixels of different views in terms of the same physic point of the inspected part is not a trivial step, especially for a texture-less object, such as a piece of white paper. Another problem is the sparse resolution of the reconstruction, usually with a small number of points. Furthermore, the inappropriate ambient light condition would also lead to the failure of the passive stereo vision.

In order to overcome the above drawbacks, active stereo vision, removing the ambiguity of the texture-less part with a special projection device, is commonly used when dense reconstructions are needed. For this technique, a special device (e.g. projector) is employed to emit special patterns onto the identified object, which will be detected by the camera.

In a word, compared with the passive strategy, the active one is advantageous for robust and accurate 3D scene reconstruction.

This chapter summarizes the coding strategy, 3D reconstruction, and sensor calibration for active stereo vision, as well as the specific application in manufacturing industry. Our contribution is to propose two pattern coding strategies and pixel-to-pixel calibration for accurate 3D reconstruction in industrial inspection.

2. Coding strategy

2.1 Related work

The key of the active stereo vision method is the encoding of the structured light pattern, used to establish the correspondence between the camera and the projector, since it would impact all the system performance, including measurement accuracy, the density of point cloud, perception speed and reliability.

This chapter will focus on the fast 3D profile management. For this purpose we only summarize the coding strategies with a single and a few patterns. A great variety of different patterns have been addressed during the past decades(Salvi et al., 2010), e.g., temporal-coding patterns, direct-coding patterns, and spatial-neighborhood patterns, among which the temporal-coding patterns are multi-shot and the other two patterns are one-shot.

For the temporal-coding approach, a group of patterns are sequentially illuminated onto the measured surface. The codeword of each pixel is usually generated by its own intensity variance over time. Therefore, this approach is usually regarded as a pixel-independent and multiplexed approach. Because of the high accuracy and resolution performance, the temporal patterns are the most extensively employed method in optical metrology.

At present, the phase-shifting method (PSM), which is a typical example of the above temporal patterns, is the most commonly used pattern in 3D profile measurement for industrial quality inspection. The reason is that this method could reach pixel-level resolution with high density. Another benefit of this technique is its robustness to surface reflectivity and ambient light variations. For this technique, the minimum number of patterns required is three. Hence, a three-step phase shifting pattern is usually used, in which three sinusoidal patterns with $2\pi/3$ phase shifting relative to each other are utilized (Huang & Zhang, 2006).

However, the calculated phase distribution is constricted in the rage of $\left[-\pi \; +\pi\right)$ by means of anti-tangent function due to the periodic property of the sinusoidal waveform, which is named relative phase. Therefore, it is necessary to determine the order of phase shifting in the camera image plane to eliminate the ambiguity, in order to obtain the absolute phase, which refers to the continuous phase value relative to the standard phase.

The absolute phase φ_{a} is usually expressed using the relative phase φ_{r} as

$$\varphi_{\mathrm{a}} = \varphi_{\mathrm{r}} + 2k\pi \tag{1}$$

where k is the order of phase shifting. Furthermore, the relationship between the absolute phase φ_{a} and the relative phase φ_{r} can be demonstrated as in figure 1.

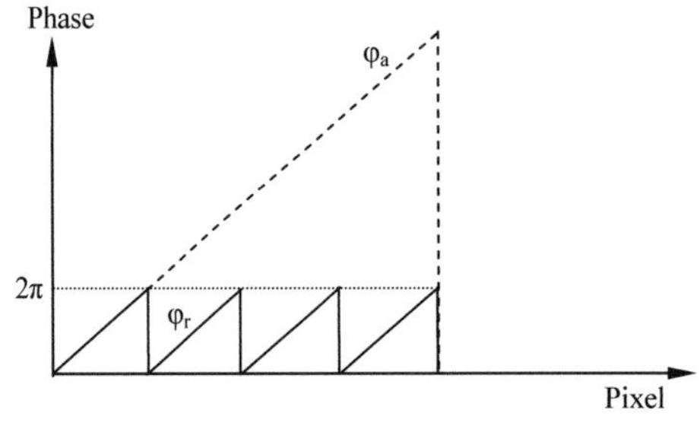

Fig. 1. The relationship between absolute phase and relative phase

To solve this problem, several unwrapping algorithms have been developed (Ghiglia & Pritt, 1998), among which a general unwrapping algorithm is to introduce a marker, i.e., a line in the perpendicular direction of the phase distribution. In this case, the absolute phase with respect to the reference marker can be obtained by using the assumption of continuity of the measured object. Several similar strategies have also been developed to solve this problem. It should be pointed out that the proposed algorithms can only be used for smooth surfaces with height variation no more than 2π within any adjacent pixels. Therefore, the 2π ambiguity problem will arise when measuring surfaces with abrupt steps, resulting in inaccuracy of the 3D measurement. Increasing the wavelength of phase shifting can solve this problem; however, the measurement accuracy will be affected and the system will be susceptible to noise.

One feasible solution is to take advantage of gray code and phase-shifting (GCPS) methods. The gray code is essentially a binary code in which only two intensity levels are used. Moreover, the constraint of Hamming distance is applied in the codeword formulation in the gray code method. Thus, this technique is robust to noise. The basic idea of the GCPS method is to divide the entire image plane into small patches by using the gray code method to remove the 2π discontinuities; and then determine the fine relative phase in each patch (a measured modulo 2π) by using the phase-shifting method. Thus, by integrating the gray code and phase-shifting methods, the GCPS method achieves high accuracy and removes the 2π ambiguity (Sansoni et al., 1999).

In addition to the GCPS method, an alternative way to resolve the above phase ambiguity problem is the multiple-wavelength phase-shifting method (Towers et al., 2005; Reich et al., 1997) as shown in figure 2. In this method, at least two different phase shifting patterns with wavelengths λ_a and λ_b are used to distinguish the phase shifting order by comparing the phase difference in an extended range with an equivalent wavelength λ_{ab}, which can be specified as:

$$\lambda_{ab} = \frac{\lambda_a \lambda_b}{\lambda_b - \lambda_a} \tag{2}$$

The extended wavelength leads to a unique phase distribution for the entire image without loss of accuracy.

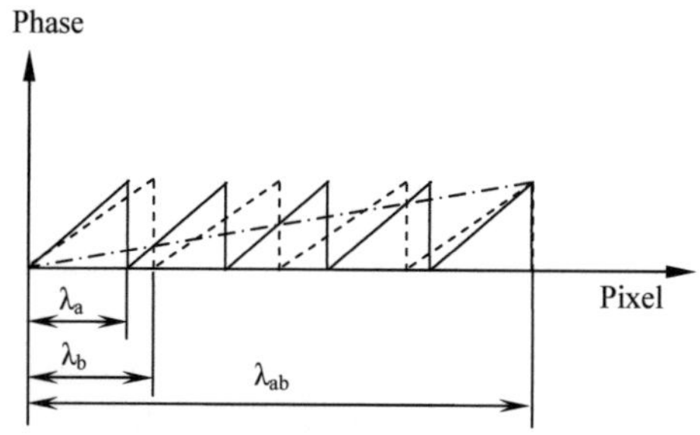

Fig. 2. Phase shifting with multiple-wavelength

However, both the GCPS method and the multiple-wavelength phase-shifting method require more structured light patterns, which will sacrifice the measurement speed. Meanwhile, these methods can only be used to measure stationary parts; otherwise, the sensor may capture non-corresponding pattern codes due to the displacement of the inspected target, resulting in inaccurate 3D shape measurement.

To reduce the number of patterns, a feasible solution is to integrate multiple phase shifting patterns into a single composite pattern for real-time measurement (Guan et al., 2003), at the expense of measurement accuracy. Another commonly used one-shot pattern strategy is based on the Fourier Transform Profilometry (FTP) (Takeda & Mutoh, 1983), in which a single pattern is projected and analyzed in the spatial frequency domain. It should be noted that the spectrum aliasing phenomena will affect the measurement accuracy. It should be mentioned that a common problem of the phase shifting methods is their susceptibility to sensor and environment noise.

In the direct-coding approach, to achieve a pixel level resolution, each pixel should have a unique color value in the same pattern. Thus, a great number of colors are required. Moreover, the captured color by the camera does not only depends on the color of the projected pattern, but also relies on the color of the scanned surface. Thus, this direct-coding technique is very susceptible to noise and ambient light and is inappropriate for quality inspection.

In the spatial-neighborhood approach, the codeword of the primitive is specified by its own value and the values of its adjacent primitives. Thus, this technique can be implemented in one-shot pattern for real-time 3D profile measurement. The most commonly used primitives are color and geometry. Some of the color-based patterns are colored slit pattern, colored stripe pattern, colored grid pattern, colored spot pattern, etc (Tehrani et al., 2008; Pages et al., 2004; Je et al., 2004; Salvi, 1998; Payeur, 2009). The codeword of the each primitive is usually formulated under the constraint of De Bruijn sequence(Pages et al., 2004), pseudorandom sequence(Payeur, 2009) or M-arrays(Salvi, 1998). As a well-known type of mathematical sequence, the De Bruijn sequence of order m with q different symbols is a circular sequence with the length of q^m, where each subsequence of length m exactly emerges once. Thus, each subsequence can be uniquely identified in the entire sequence. Similarly, a pseudorandom sequence is generated in the same way without the subsequence formed by 0. It is noted that both of the above two methods are one-dimension spatial coding approaches, whereas M-arrays are the two-dimension coding strategy. Assume that the total number of primitives in the pattern is $\mathrm{m} \times \mathrm{n}$, and then the sub-window of $\mathrm{u} \times \mathrm{v}$ appears only once for M-arrays coding strategy. Examples of the geometry-based patterns are given in (Doignon, 2005).

Besides, the temporal monochromatic black/white stripe pattern is also usually adopted for high speed 3D shape measurement. The black/white pattern has the following advantages: first, the pattern identification is very easy and fast due to the simple image processing; second, the measurement is very reliable because of the robustness to the varied reflection property and ambient light. A temporal stripe coded pattern uses four different patterns for binary boundary code, and generates $2^8 = 256$ codes. Then, only 111 available codes are employed to avoid decode error(Rusinkiewicz, 2002).

Recently, several other coding strategies for real-time measurement have been reported. The black/white stripes combined with traversed color lines are used to form one-shot patterns. In this method, the epipolar geometry constraint is used to decode the intersections between the stripe boundaries and the color lines(Koninckx & Gool, 2006). A single stripe pattern is proposed to reconstruct the 3D human face. To clarify the index of each stripe, an algorithm based on the maximum spanning tree of a graph is used to identify the potential connectivity and the adjacency in recorded stripes(Brink et al., 2008).

For accurate, reliable and fast measurements of industrial parts (e.g., automotive parts), the projection pattern is supposed to meet the following requirements:

(a) high robustness to the reflectivity variance of the measured part;

(b) high consistence of the measurement performance;

(c) appropriate point cloud density to represent the 3D shape;

(d) accurate location of the primitives;

(e) rapid decoding capability.
Motivated by these facts, we developed two novel structured light patterns for rapid 3D measurement(Xu et al., 2010; 2011), inspired by previous research.
The first one, X-point pattern, is a one-shot pattern based on geometrical feature and neighboring information. The primitive of this pattern is the corner of the black/white chessboard pattern. Compared with traditional geometric primitives, such as disc and stripe, the primitive of the X-point pattern is more reliable and accurate in detecting the primitive's location. The value of the primitive is represented by the direction of the X-point. This X-point pattern can be used for real-time 3D shape measurement thanks to its one-shot nature.
The second one, the two-level binary pattern strategy, makes use of both the temporal and spatial coding to reduce the number of required patterns. In this method, the value of the stripe boundary (primitive) is determined by the intensity variance in time domain. Then, the codeword of the primitive is calculated by using its own value and the values of the neighboring primitives in space domain. This is the reason why this method is termed as "two-level pattern" in this chapter.

2.2 X-point pattern coding strategy

The X-point pattern is based on the black/white binary pattern, through which the system robustness can be enhanced by removing the influence of the color property of the inspected parts. Only the geometrical feature can be used to distinguish different primitives in the pattern when using this method. The concept of the X-point method is derived from the chessboard, which is usually used in camera calibration due to the accurate positioning of corner points. Thus, the X-point method is very accurate for 3D measurement. The value of the primitive is represented by its orientation. As shown in figure 3, the corresponding values of the four primitives are denoted as 0, 1, 2, and 3, respectively. The angle between the orientation of the primitive and the horizontal line are 0, 45, 90, and 135 degrees, respectively.

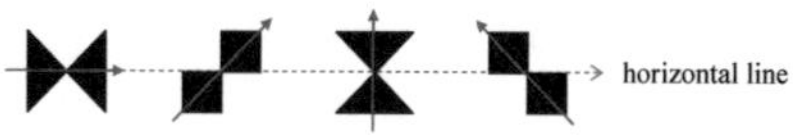

Fig. 3. The primitive design

Apparently, these four primitives are inadequate to remove the ambiguity in the pattern. To solve this problem, the neighboring coding information should be integrated to obtain much more amount of codeword. A straight-forward solution is to use both the value of a primitive and those of its eight neighboring primitives, as shown in figure 4. In this case, the pattern is able to recognize the $4^9 = 262,144$ unique primitives. Therefore, the maximum-allowable number of points in the proposed pattern is 262,144 in theory.
Another benefit of the X-point method is to decrease occlusion influences. As shown in figure 5, a primitive located on the edge of the inspected part usually leads to partial loss of the geometrical shape. However, it is evident that the primitive can still be detected by using the proposed method, resulting in improved system performance.

2.3 Two-level binary pattern coding strategy

Similarly, the two-level coding strategy is also based on the black/white pattern, to improve reliability. Furthermore, the pattern is a three-step pattern, i.e. , the number of patterns is three for 3D profile measurement. In this approach, the codeword of the primitive is determined by

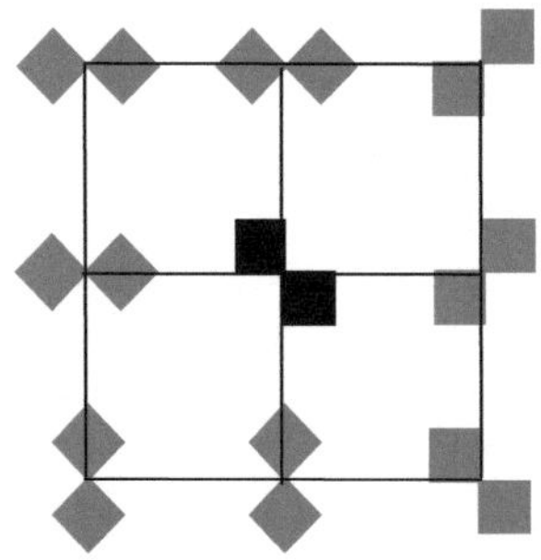

Fig. 4. The codeword based on 8 neighbor

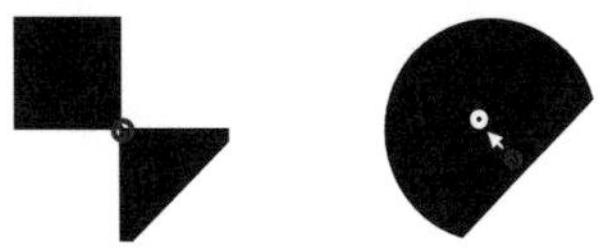

Fig. 5. An example of occlusion

its own value and those of the neighboring primitives. The method to generate the boundary value (represented by intensity variation in time domain) of two adjacent stripes is presented as follows.

In theory, the maximum possible number of intensity variance for each stripe over time is eight. In this chapter, the values are represented by 000, 001, 010, 011, 100, 101, 110, and 111, respectively. The value 001 means that the intensity of the stripe is switched in the order of white, black, and black over time. In this chapter, the values 000 and 111 are discarded to remove the influence of the reflectivity of the inspected part. In other words, the intensity of the stripe should change at least once during the measurement. Therefore, six remaining values 001, 010, 011, 100, 101, and 110 are used for coding the stripe. In order to achieve sub-pixel accuracy of stripe boundary detection, the location is specified by using the inverse intensity stripe, as shown in figure 6. A, B, C and D represent the intensity values of the successive pixels n and $n+1$ around the stripe boundary. The accurate location of a stripe boundary can be obtained as:

$$P = P_{n+1} - \frac{D - B}{(A + D) - (B + C)} \tag{3}$$

It is clear that the error is constrained within one pixel by using the above approach.

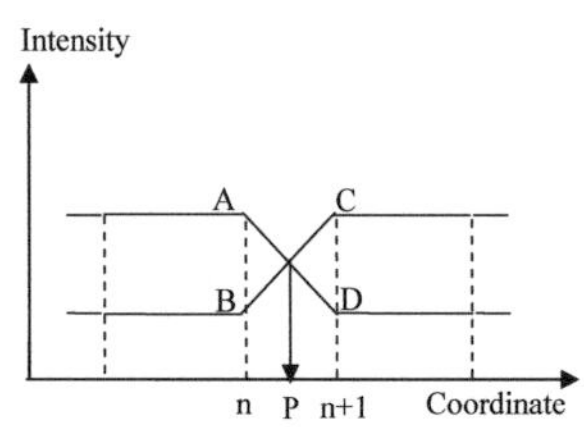

Fig. 6. The edge detection with inverse intensity

The above stripe boundary detection strategy imports another constraint for the configuration of adjacent stripes, where the intensity is supposed to vary twice in the space domain. In this case, assuming that one stripe is 001, the next stripe can only be selected from 010, 100, 110. Thus, the possible number for the arrangement of connected stripes is $3 \times 6 = 18$. The potential stripe boundaries are listed in figure 7

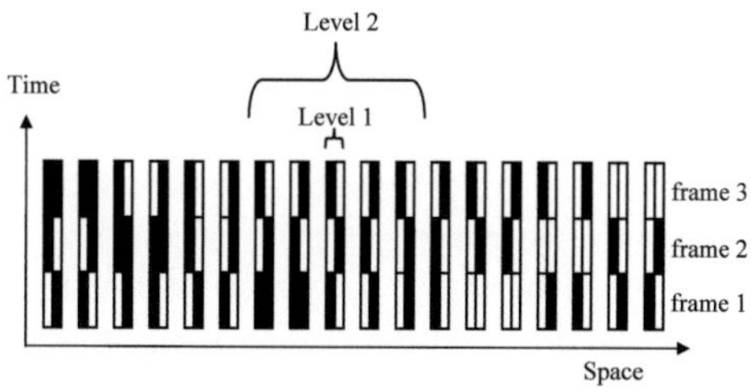

Fig. 7. The potential stripe boundaries

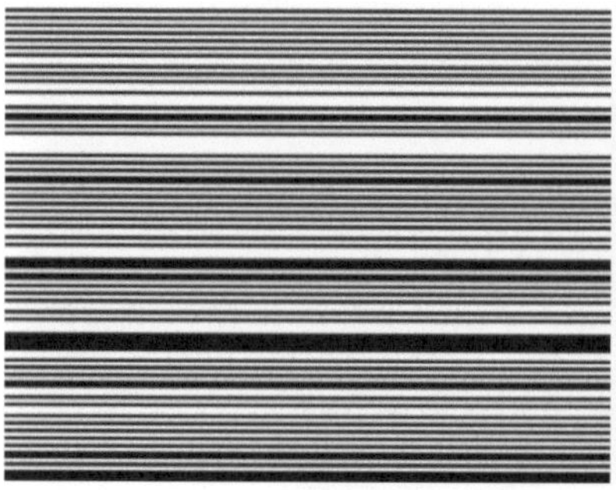

(a) Pattern 1

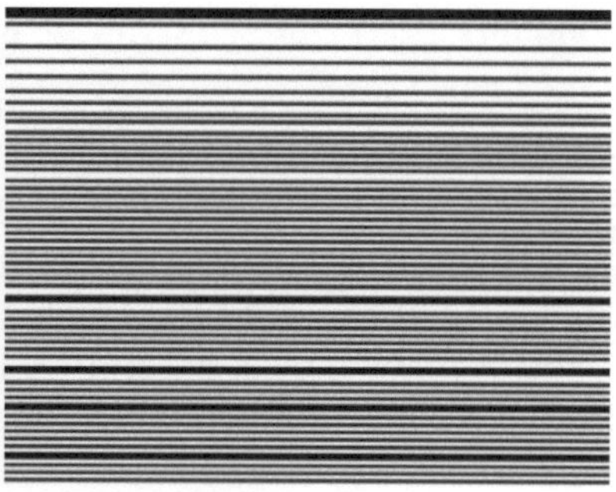

(b) Pattern 2

(c) Pattern 3

Fig. 8. The three two-level patterns

The second step is to form the codeword for each stripe boundary by using a series of successive stripes in space. Thus, the two-level pattern is essentially a sequence of stripe patterns. The codeword of each stripe boundary is determined by a successive subsequence. To uniquely locate each stripe boundary in a single pattern, the subsequence length n should be specified. Without loss of generality, we assume that the possible number of the first stripe is 6 while the possible number of the second one is 3. Similarly, there are 3 options for each stripe in the remaining adjacent stripes. Therefore, the number of unique subsequence is $6 \times 3^{n-1}$. For instance, if the length of the subsequence is 4, then 162 unique subsequences can be formulated under the above constraints. The subsequence can be generated by using

Fleury's algorithm, which is described in detail in (Xu et al., 2011). 128 unique subsequences are selected to form the illuminated patterns for 3D profile measurement, The pattern resolution is 768×1024 pixels, where the width of each strip is 6 pixels as shown in figure 8.

3. Phase-height mapping strategy

The phase-height mapping approach is the critical step of active vision, which converts the phase distribution in the camera image plane to the corresponding coordinate of the inspected object. The existing methods for transforming the phase to coordinate can be categorized into two types: absolute height method and relative height method.

In a stereo vision sensor, the projector is considered as an inverse camera, thus, both the camera and the projector can be represented by the pinhole model. When the distortion of the lens is ignored, the relationship between a point of the scanned object in the world frame and the corresponding pixels in the camera or projector image plane can be uniformly expressed:

$$sI = A\left[R\ t\right]X \tag{4}$$

where $I = \left[r\ c\ 1\right]^T$ is the homogeneous coordinate of any arbitrary pixel in the image frame of the camera or projector; $X = \left[x\ y\ z\ 1\right]^{\mathrm{T}}$ is the homogeneous coordinate of the corresponding point in the world frame; s is a scale factor; $\left[R\ t\right]$ is the extrinsic parameters representing the 3×3 rotation matrix and 3×1 translation vector from the world frame to the image frame; A is the intrinsic parameters matrix which is written as:

$$A = \begin{bmatrix} \alpha\ \gamma\ r_0 \\ 0\ \beta\ c_0 \\ 0\ 0\ 1 \end{bmatrix} \tag{5}$$

Where r_0 and c_0 are the coordinates of the principle point; α and β are the focal length along two image axes of the image plane; γ is the skew parameter of the two image axes. Further, Eq.(4) can be represented by using the perspective projection matrix:

$$s\begin{bmatrix} r \\ c \\ 1 \end{bmatrix} = \begin{bmatrix} m_{11}\ m_{12}\ m_{13}\ m_{14} \\ m_{21}\ m_{22}\ m_{23}\ m_{24} \\ m_{31}\ m_{32}\ m_{33}\ m_{34} \end{bmatrix} \begin{bmatrix} x \\ y \\ z \\ 1 \end{bmatrix} \tag{6}$$

where $\begin{bmatrix} m_{11}\ m_{12}\ m_{13}\ m_{14} \\ m_{21}\ m_{22}\ m_{23}\ m_{24} \\ m_{31}\ m_{32}\ m_{33}\ m_{34} \end{bmatrix} = A\left[R\ t\right] = M$ is is the perspective projection matrix, which is utilized to map a 3D point in the word frame to a 2D point in the image plane.

Next, we eliminate the homogeneous scale s in Eq. (6) and obtain the general formula for both the camera and projector as:

$$\begin{cases} r = \frac{m_{11}x+m_{12}y+m_{13}z+m_{14}}{m_{31}x+m_{32}y+m_{33}z+m_{34}} \\ c = \frac{m_{21}x+m_{22}y+m_{23}z+m_{24}}{m_{31}x+m_{32}y+m_{33}z+m_{34}} \end{cases} \tag{7}$$

Without loss of generality, any pixel in the camera image plane generates a viewing ray-line through the optical center of the camera in the world frame. Then, we can obtain the viewing ray-line equation by using the following liner equation:

$$\begin{cases} r^c = \frac{m_{11}^c x + m_{12}^c y + m_{13}^c z + m_{14}^c}{m_{31}^c x + m_{32}^c y + m_{33}^c z + m_{34}^c} \\ c^c = \frac{m_{21}^c x + m_{22}^c y + m_{23}^c z + m_{24}^c}{m_{31}^c x + m_{32}^c y + m_{33}^c z + m_{34}^c} \end{cases} \tag{8}$$

Moreover, we can get the absolute phase distribution when the stripe pattern (i.e., two-level binary pattern) or the phase shifting pattern is adopted. In this case, the corresponding pixel in the projector image plane must lie on a line with the same phase value. To be specific, we assume that the line is a horizontal line with coordinate c_p, thus, the line forms a projecting ray-plane through the optical center of the projector in the world frame, intersecting the scanned surface.

$$c^p = \frac{m_{21}^p x + m_{22}^p y + m_{23}^p z + m_{24}^p}{m_{31}^p x + m_{32}^p y + m_{33}^p z + m_{34}^p} \tag{9}$$

Obviously, the scanned surface point is the intersection of the ray-plane and the ray-line as shown in figure 9 by using linear equations bringing the Eq.(8) and Eq.(9) together. So this method is referred to as the plane-line mapping approach in this chapter.

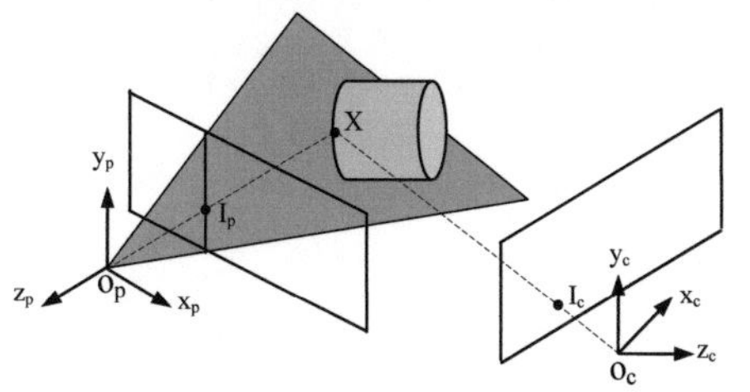

Fig. 9. The intersection of the plane and line

Actually, the projector is regarded as an inverse camera, since it projects images instead of capturing them. Consequently, both the camera and the projector have the same mathematic model such that the epipolar constraint is also satisfied by the projector and the camera. As shown in figure 10, point X is a measured point of the distorted stripe boundary on the inspected part. Point I_c is the projection of X in the camera image plane; while point I_p is the corresponding point of X in the projector image plane. Thus, the point I_p is restricted to lie on the epipolar line l_p due to the constraint of the epipolar geometry in stereo vision:

$$l_p = F \cdot I_c \tag{10}$$

where F is the fundamental matrix determined by calibration.

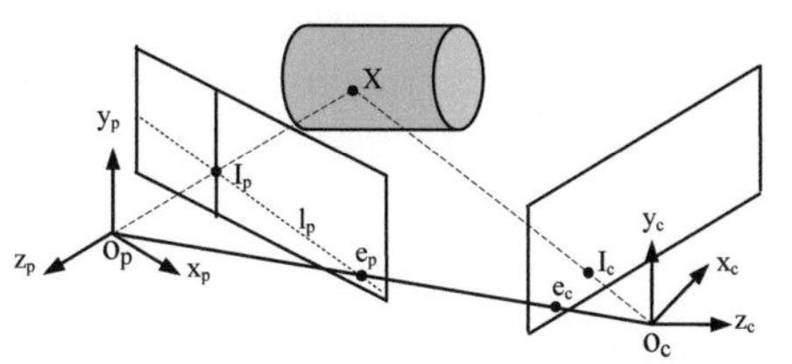

Fig. 10. The intersection of the line and line

When the stripe pattern or the phase shifting pattern is used, the corresponding pixel I_p for pixel I_c in the camera plane is the intersection the epipolar line l_p and the line with the phase equal to that of I_c in the projector plane.

Similarly, if the two-dimension coding pattern (i.e, X-point pattern), providing the location in the two axes of projector image plane, is adopted, then the pixel I_p can be directly obtained without the help of epipolar geometry.
Once the corresponding pixels are determined, we can get the a projecting ray-line through the optical center of the projector as:

$$\begin{cases} r^c = \frac{m_{11}^c x + m_{12}^c y + m_{13}^c z + m_{14}^c}{m_{31}^c x + m_{32}^c y + m_{33}^c z + m_{34}^c} \\ c^c = \frac{m_{21}^c x + m_{22}^c y + m_{23}^c z + m_{24}^c}{m_{31}^c x + m_{32}^c y + m_{33}^c z + m_{34}^c} \end{cases} \tag{11}$$

In this case, the calculation of the 3D surface point is converted to a line-line intersection problem. Combining Eq.(8) and Eq.(11), we can get the coordinate of the surface point. The equation can be solved by using the least-squares method, however, due to errors in the pinhole model of the camera and projector, the two ray-lines will not intersect in the 3D space. A better way is to compute the closest approach of the two skew lines, i.e., the shortest line segment connecting them. If the length of this segment is less than the threshold, we assign the midpoints as the intersection of the two lines; if it is larger than the threshold, we assume that there are some mistakes for the correspondence. The elaborated description for this method can be found in (Shapiro, 2001).

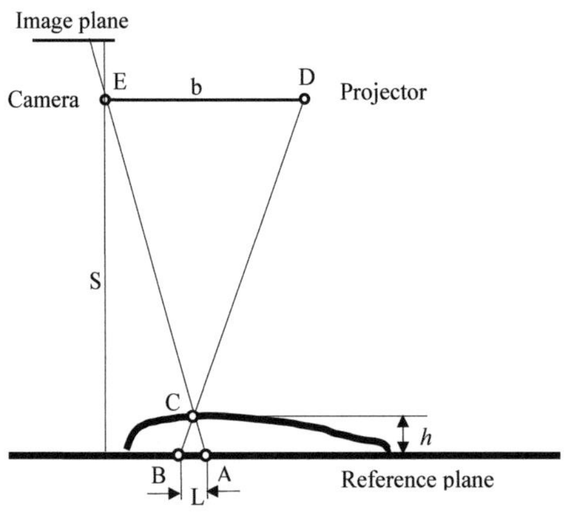

Fig. 11. The relative height caculation

Instead of measuring the absolute coordinate, the relative height variation is more emphasized in quality inspections. So another method is to obtain the relative height with respect to the reference plane using the triangular similarity method. As shown in figure 11, from the similar triangles ΔABC and ΔCDE , the relative height h from the surface to the reference plane can be calculated by

$$h = \frac{L \times S}{b + L} \tag{12}$$

where b denotes the baseline distance between the optical centers of the camera and projector; S is the standoff distance between the reference plane and the optical center of the camera; L is the distance of two corresponding pixels A and B. Eq.(12) can be further rewritten by using the pixel coordinate as:

$$h = \frac{res \times m \times S}{b + res \times m} \tag{13}$$

in which *res* is the resolution of the camera with a unit of mm/pixel and m signifies the number of pixels from A to B.
Furthermore, a simplified calculation of the relative height can be directly expressed as the production of a coefficient and the phase when the stand off distance S is much larger than the relative height h. (Su et al., 1992)

4. Calibration

The key procedure to guarantee accurate profile reconstruction of the inspected object is the proper calibration of the components of the active stereo vision, involving camera, projector, and system calibration(Li & Chen, 2003). The fundamental difference between the passive stereo vision and the active stereo vision is that one camera is replaced by a projector, leading to time-consuming and complicated calibration procedure for the reason that the projector cannot directly view the scene. To solve this problem, the projector is treated as an inverse camera. Then, we can calibrate the camera and the projector separately. We fist calibrate the camera and then determine the correspondence between the pixels in the projector and those in the calibration gauge using the camera(Zhang & Huang, 2006). In this case, the projector can be calibrated by using a similar technique as camera calibration. To be specific, the calibration of intrinsic and extrinsic parameters of both camera and projector can be implemented by using in the online Matalab toolbox.
Other methods involve neural networks, bundle adjustment, or absolute phase. However, these traditional calibration methods for active stereo vision treat both the camera and the projector as pin-hole models. A pinhole model is an ideal mathematical model where all the incident light rays go through a single point. However, a calibration residual error always exist when using a pinhole model, especially for affordable off-the-shelf equipment.
In this chapter, a pixel-to-pixel calibration concept has been adopted to improve system accuracy. For this technique, pixel-wise correspondence between the projector and the camera is established, instead of using the unique transformation matrix as in the approach mentioned above. Therefore, the significant merit is to improve the measurement accuracy because of the elimination of residual error of the sensor calibration. Additionally, another advantage is to avoid the projector calibration, which appears more tedious and complicated since the projector cannot view the calibration gauge in the scene.
From Eq. (13), the motivation of the active stereo vision sensor calibration is to obtain the parameters S, b and *res*. First, we will explain how to calibrate the parameter (S, b) for each couple of corresponding points in the pixel-to-pixel calibration approach.
In figure 12, the points D_i and E_i are corresponding pixels belonging to the same physical point C_i, where E_i, a virtual point, perhaps out of the image plane of the camera, is the intersection of two lines: the reflective ray of light C_iE_i , and the baseline D_iE_i parallel to the reference plane. In this case, a set of sensor parameter matrices $\left(b_{(i,j)}, S_{(i,j)}, i = 1, 2 \cdots m; j = 1, 2 \cdots n\right)$ are required to be calculated for each point on the projector image plane, where i, j are image coordinate indices of the correspondences in camera. A group of $L_{n(i,j)}$ can be calculated while the reference plane is moved to different heights for n times. Consequently, the sensor parameters $b_{(i,j)}$ and $S_{(i,j)}$ are computed using a linear least squares approach:

$$\begin{bmatrix} h_{1(i,j)} & -L_{1(i,j)} \\ \cdots & \cdots \\ h_{n(i,j)} & -L_{n(i,j)} \end{bmatrix} \cdot \begin{bmatrix} b_{(i,j)} \\ S_{(i,j)} \end{bmatrix} = \begin{bmatrix} -h_{1(i,j)} \times L_{1(i,j)} \\ \cdots \\ -h_{n(i,j)} \times L_{n(i,j)} \end{bmatrix} \tag{14}$$

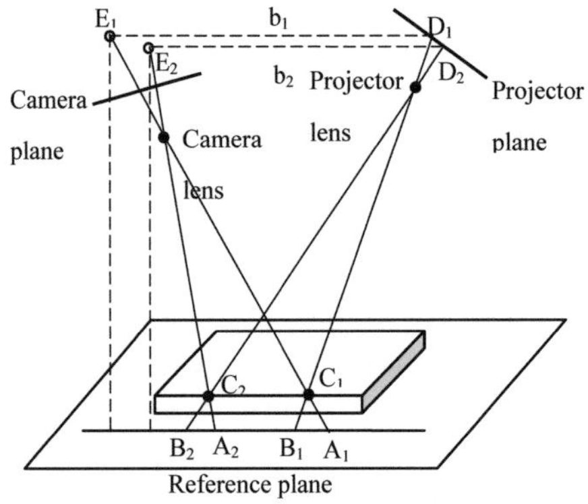

Fig. 12. Calibration of parameter (S, b)

So, Eqn.(12) can be rewritten as

$$h_{(i,j)} = \frac{L_{(i,j)} \times S_{(i,j)}}{b_{(i,j)} + L_{(i,j)}} \tag{15}$$

The remaining parameter *res* can be obtained by counting the pixels of a line with known length in the image. Next, the distance L can be further determined by using the calibrated parameter *res*.

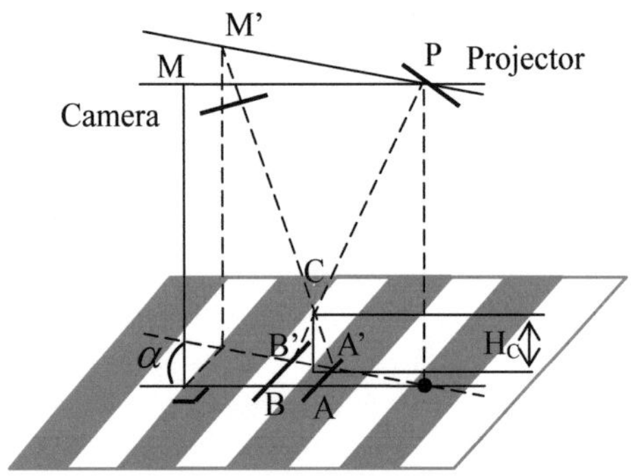

Fig. 13. Calibration of the offset angle α

The previous discussion focuses on the calibration the baseline distance b and standoff S provided that the L is accurately measured. However, inaccurate placement of the camera and projector will generate a system offset angle α, resulting in error of L, As shown in figure 13, point C is the point on the surface of the inspected object, with relative height H_C to the reference plane. AB and $A'B'$ are the projected lines of MP and $M'P$ on the reference plane, respectively. The calculated line AB is perpendicular to the stripe boundary. The angle between the calculated line AB and actual line $A'B'$ is called the offset angle α, which has to be calibrated. When using a pixel-to-pixel calibration method, M is assumed point corresponding to P. However actually M' is the real point corresponding to point P. $\Delta M'CP$ and $\Delta A'CB'$ are similar triangles and hence the distance L' between point A' and B' should be used to compute H_C. However, the patterns used are encoded along the image rows, which means codes are identical in one dimension. If α is not calibrated, instead of L', L will be

utilized to calculate H_C Therefore, the error ΔL between L' and L causes the error ΔH_C in measuring H_C.
To solve this problem, one way is to encode both horizontal and vertical stripes, which requires much more time for image acquisition and processing. An alternative method is to calibrate the offset angle ΔL in off-line mode, speeding up the real-time inspection process. The real distance $L'_{(i,j)}$ can be denoted by:

$$L'_{(i,j)} = L_{(i,j)} \sec\left(\alpha_{(i,j)}\right) \tag{16}$$

where $L_{(i,j)}$ is the is the measured distance and $\alpha_{(i,j)}$ is calibrated offset angle.
Similarly to the baseline and standoff distance calibration, the offset angle $\alpha_{(i,j)}$ also can be calibrated by pixel-to-pixel strategy. The calibration procedure can be divided into two steps:
(1)Determine a pair of corresponding points A' and C' from two sets of images
(2)Calculate the offset angle $\alpha_{(i,j)}$

5. Experimental results and discussion

A prototype of a 3D shape rapid measurement system, as shown in figure 14, has been developed to verify the performance of the two proposed coding strategies, based on X-point and two-level binary patterns. For the larger scale part measurement, in order to ensure that the covered area for each pixel is not too big for the accuracy requirement, four groups of area sensors are configured. Each area sensor consists of a commercial projector (Hitachi CP-X253 Series LCD Projectors, with 768 × 1024 resolution) and a high resolution commercial IEEE-1394 monochrome camera (Toshiba Monochrome Firewire Cameras with 2008 × 2044 resolution, Model: CSB4000F-10). The baseline distance (distance of the optical centers between the camera and projector) of the area sensor is around 500 mm and the standoff distance(distance between the reference plane and the optical center of the camera) is approximate 1550 mm. The exact values of baseline distance and standoff distance are calibrated using the proposed pixel-to-pixel method.

Fig. 14. The measurement system setup

The first experiment is to evaluate the accuracy of the measurement system, where a known-height flat gauge is measured 10 times by the X-point pattern and the two-level

binary pattern separately. The standard deviation shows the accuracy and consistency of the measurement performance. For our measurement system, the standard deviations of the X-point pattern and two-level binary pattern were 0.18 mm and 0.19 mm, respectively. The results illustrate that the two proposed patterns have similar accuracy performances. It should be stressed that the accuracy can be further improved if the baseline distance is extended. However, the negative impact of this is that the measurement area is decreased because of the reduction of the common field of view for the projector and camera.
The second experiment is to validate the efficiency of the proposed patterns for complicated part measurements. To this end, two different automotive parts (a pillar with a size of around 700×550 mm and a door with a size of around 1500×750 mm) with different shapes were used in our trials. The results as shown in figure 15 demonstrate that the proposed patterns can handle the step of the pillar and the hole of the door even when occlusion arises.

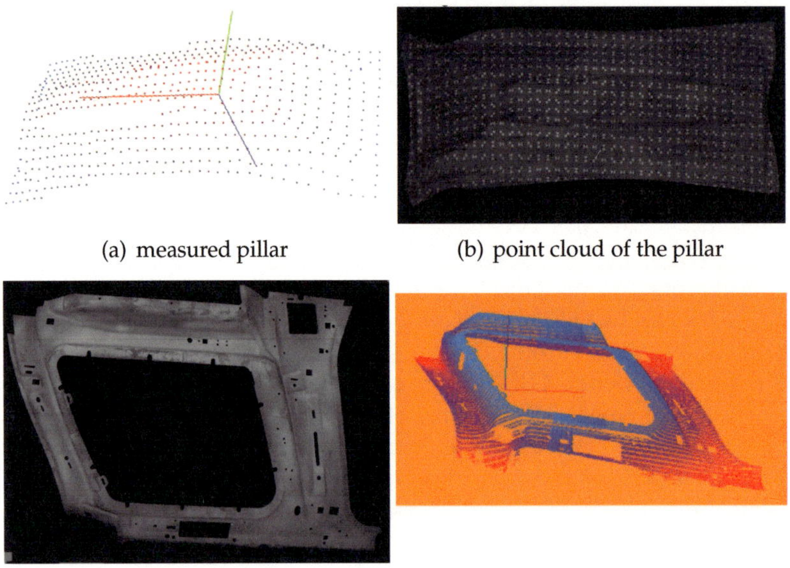

(a) measured pillar (b) point cloud of the pillar

(c) measured door (d) point cloud of the door

Fig. 15. The complicated part measurement

6. Conclusion

The purpose of this chapter has been to introduce the measurement system based on active stereo vision. The pattern coding strategy is the most important for active stereo vision. Therefore, we first summarized the existing strategies for the 3D rapid measurement. To meet the requirements of industrial quality inspection, two black/white patterns, including X-point and two-level stripe patterns, have been proposed in this chapter. Both patterns can provide the absolute phase distribution, useful for the parts with complicated shapes(e.g., the step and the hole). The experimental results demonstrate that the proposed patterns promise high speed, robustness and accuracy. To increase the accuracy of the measurement system and avoid the need for projector calibration, a pixel-to-pixel calibration approach has been employed in this chapter. The common shortcoming of our proposed patterns is the lack of pixel-wise resolution, which can be obtained by using phase shifting. In the future, a coding strategy of higher resolution, requiring less patterns, will be studied.

7. Acknowledgements

This publication was supported by National Science Foundation of China (NSFC), Grant 50975148, 51005126. As well, the authors would like to thank Jing Xu's former supervisor Dr. Xi Ning at Michigan State University. Most of work was performed under his support. The authors also thank Dr. Shi Quan from PPG Industries Inc. for his brilliant work and cooperation.

8. References

Longuet-Higgins, H. C. (1981). A computer algorithm for reconstructing a scene from two projections. *Nature*, Vol.293, (September 1981),(133-135)

Salvi, J.; Fernandez, S.; Pribanic, T & Llado, X. (2010). A state of the art in structured light patterns for surface profilometry. *Pattern Recognition*, Vol.43, No. 4. (August 2010), pp.2666-2680

Huang, P. S. & Zhang, S. (2006). Fast three-step phase-shifting algorithm. *Applied Optics*, Vol. 45, No. 21, (July 2006), pp.5086-5091

Ghiglia, D. C. & Pritt, M. D. (1998). *Two-Dimensional Phase Unwrapping: Theory, Algorithms, and Software*, Wiley-Interscience, ISBN 0471249351, Gaithersburg, Maryland, US.

Sansoni, G.; Carocci, M. & Rodella R. (1999). Three-dimensional vision based on a combination of gray-code and phase-shift light projection: analysis and compensation of the systematic errors. *Applied Optics*, Vol. 38, No. 31, (November 1999), pp.6565-6573.

Towers, C. E.; Towers, D. P. & Jones J. D. C. (2005). Absolute fringe order calculation using optimised multi-frequency selection in full-field profilometry. *Optics and Lasers in Engineering*, Vol. 43, No. 7, (July 2005), pp.788ÍC800.

Reich, C.; Ritter, R. & Thesing J.. (1997). White light heterodyne principle for 3D-measurement, *SPIE Proceedings of Sensors, Sensor Systems, and Sensor Data Processing*, pp. 236-344, Munich, Germany, June 1997.

Guan, C.; Hassebrook, L. G. &Lau, D. L. (2003). Composite structured light pattern for three-dimensional video. *Optics Express*, Vol. 11, No. 5, (March 2003), pp.406-417.

Takeda M, & Mutoh K. (1983). Fourier transform profilometry for the automatic measurement 3-D object shapes. *Applied Optics*, Vol. 22, No. 24, pp.3977-3982.

Tehrani, M.; Saghaeian, A. & Mohajerani, O. (2008). A new approach to 3D modeling using structured light pattern, *3rd International Conference on Information and Communication Technologies:From Theory to Applications,ICTTA*, pp. 1ÍC5, Damascus, Syria, April 7-11, 2008

Pages, J.; Salvi, J. & Forest, J. (2004). A New Optimized De Bruijn Coding Strategy for Structured Light Patterns, *17th International Conference on Pattern Recognition, ICPR*, pp.284-287, Cambridge, UK, 23-26 August 2004.

Je, C.; Lee, S. W. & Park, R. (2004). High-Contrast Color-Stripe Pattern for Rapid Structured-Light Range Imaging, *8th European Conference on Computer Vision, ECCV*, pp.95-107, Prague, Czech Republic, May 11-14, 2004.

Zhang, L.; Curless, B. & Seitz S. M. (2002). Rapid Shape Acquisition Using Color Structured Light and Multi-pass Dynamic Programming, *3D data processing visualization transmission, 3DPVT*, pp.24-37, Padova Italy June 19-21 2002 .

Salvi, J.; Pages, J. & Batlle, J. (1998). A robust-coded pattern projection for dynamic 3D scene measurement. *Pattern Recognition Letters*, Volume 19, Issue 11, September 1998, Pp 1055-1065

Payeur, P. & Desjardins, D. (2009). Structured Light Stereoscopic Imaging with Dynamic Pseudo-random Patterns. *International Conference on Image Analysis and Recognition*, pp.687-696, Halifax, Canada, July 6-8 2009.

Doignon, C.; Ozturk, C. & Knittel, D. (2005). A structured light vision system for out-of-plane vibration frequencies location of a moving web, *Machine vision and applications*, Vol.16, No.5 (December 2005), 289-297.

Rusinkiewicz S.; Hall-Holt, O.; &Levoy, Marc. (2006). Real-Time 3D Model Acquisition , *ACM Transactions on Graphics (TOG) - Proceedings of ACM SIGGRAPH 2002* , vol.21, No.3, (July 2002), pp.438-446.

Koninckx, T. P. & Gool, L. V.; (2006). Real-Time Range Acquisition by Adaptive Structured Light, *IEEE Transactions On Pattern Analysis ad Machine Intelligence*, VOL.28, NO.3, MARCH 2006, pp.339ÍC343.

Brink, W., Robinson, A., & Rodrigues, M., (2008). Indexing Uncoded Stripe Patterns in Structured Light Systems by Maximum Spanning Trees. *British Machine Vision Conference BMVC*, Leeds, UK, 1-4 Sep 2008

Xu, J.; Xi, N.; Zhang, C. et al. (2010). Real-time 3D shape inspection system of automotive parts based on structured light pattern. *Optics and Laser Technology*, Vol.43, (May 2010),(1-8)

Xu, J.; Xi, N.; Zhang, C. et al. (2011). Rapid 3D surface profile measurement of industrial parts using two-level structured light patterns. *Optics and Lasers in Engineering*, Vol.49, No.7, (July 2011) (907-914)

Su X. Y.; Zhou W. S.; Bally G. & Vukicevic D. (1992). Automated phase-measuring profilometry using defocused projection of a Ronchi grating . *Optics and Laser Technology*, Vol.94, No.6 (December 1992),pp.561-573

Shapiro L. G. (2001). *Computer Vision*, Prentice Hall, ISBN 0130307963, Upper Saddle River, NJ. US

Li Y. F. & Chen S. Y. (2003). Automatic recalibration of an active structured light vision system. *IEEE Transactions on Robotics and Automation*, Vol.19, No.2 (Apirl 2003),pp.259-268

Huang P. S. & Zhang, S. (2006).Novel method for structured light system calibration. *Optical Engineering*, Vol.45, No.8 (Apirl 2003),pp.259-268

2

Attentional Behaviors for Environment Modeling by a Mobile Robot

Pilar Bachiller, Pablo Bustos and Luis J. Manso
University of Extremadura
Spain

1. Introduction

Building robots capable of interacting in an effective and autonomous way with their environments requires to provide them with the ability to model the world. That is to say, the robot must interpret the environment not as a set of points, but as an organization of more complex structures with human-like meaning. Among the variety of sensory inputs that could be used to equip a robot, vision is one of the most informative ones. Through vision, the robot can analyze the appearance of objects. The use of stereo vision also gives the possibility to extract spatial information of the environment, allowing to determine the structure of the different elements composing it. However, vision suffers from some limitations when it is considered in isolation. On one hand, cameras have a limited field of view that can only be compensated through camera movements. On the other hand, the world is formed by non-convex structures that can only be interpreted by actively exploring the environment. Hence, the robot must move its head and body to give meaning to perceived elements composing its environment.

The combination of stereo vision and active exploration provides a means to model the world. While the robot explores the environment perceived regions can be clustered, forming more complex structures like walls and objects on the floor. Nevertheless, even in simple scenarios with few rooms and obstacles, the robot must be endowed with different abilities to successfully solve the task. For instance, during exploration, the robot must be able to decide where to look at while selecting where to go, avoiding obstacles and detecting what is that it is looking at. From the point of view of perception, there are different visual behaviors that take part in this process, such as those related to look towards what the robot can recognize and model, or those dedicated to maintain itself within safety limits. From the action perspective, the robot has to move in different ways depending on internal states (i.e. the status of the modeling process) and external situations (i.e. obstacles in the way to a target position). Both perception and action should influence each other in such a way that deciding where to look at depends on what the robot is doing, but also in a way that what is being perceived determines what the robot can or can not do.

Our solution to all these questions relies heavily on visual attention. Specifically, the foundation of our proposal is that attention can organize the perceptual and action processes by acting as an intermediary between both of them. The attentional connection allows, on one hand, to drive the perceptual process according to the behavioral requirements and, on the other hand, to modulate actions on the basis of the perceptual results of the attentional control. Thus, attention solves the where to look problem and, additionally, attention prevents behavioral disorganization by limiting possible actions than can be performed in a given situation. Based on this double functionality, we have developed an attention-based control scheme that generates autonomous behavior in a mobile robot endowed with a 4 dof's (degrees of freedom) stereo vision head. The proposed system is a behavioral architecture that uses attention as the connection between perception and action. Behaviors modulate the attention system according to their particular goals and generate actions consistent with the selected focus of attention. Coordination among behaviors emerges from the attentional nature of the system, so that the robot can simultaneously execute several independent, but cooperative, behaviors to reach complex goals. In this paper, we apply our control architecture to the problem of environment modeling using stereo vision by defining the attentional and behavioral components that provide the robot with the capacity to explore and model the world.

2. Environment modeling using vision

As a first approach towards the environment modeling, we focus on indoor environments composed by several rooms connected through doors. Rooms are considered approximately rectangular and may contain objects on the floor.

During exploration, perceived visual regions are stored in a 3D occupancy grid which constitutes a discrete representation of a certain zone of the environment. This occupancy grid is locally used, so, when the robot gets into a new room, the grid is reseted. Each cell of this grid contains, among other attributes, the certainty degree about the occupancy of the corresponding volume of the environment. The certainty value decreases as the distance to the perceived region increases, assuming this way possible errors in the parametrization of the stereo pair. In addition, the certainty increases as a region is perceived over time in the same position. Thus, stable regions produces higher occupancy values than unstable ones. Cells with a high certainty degree are used for detecting a room model fitting the set of perceived regions. Once the model of the current room can be considered stable, it is stored in an internal representation that maintains topological and metric information of the environment.

Several approaches on mobile robotics propose the use of topological representation to complement the metric information of the environment. In (Thrun, 1998) it is proposed to create off-line topological graphs by partitioning metric maps into regions separated by narrow passages. In (Simhon & Dudek, 1998) the environment is represented by a hybrid topological-metric map composed by a set of local metric maps called *islands of reliability*. (Tomatis et al., 2003) describes the environment using a global topological map that associates places which are metrically represented by infinite lines belonging to the same places. (Van Zwynsvoorde et al., 2000) constructs a topological representation as a route graph using Voronoï diagrams. In (Yan et al., 2006) the environment is represented by a graph whose nodes are crossings (corners or intersections). (Montijano & Sagues, 2009) organizes the information of the environment in a graph of planar regions.

In our approach, the topological representation encodes entities of higher level than the ones mentioned above. Each node of the topological graph represents a room and each edge describes a connection between two rooms. In addition, instead of maintaining a parallel metric map, each topological node contains a minimal set of metric information that allows building a metric map of a place of the environment when it is needed. This approach reduces drastically the amount of computations the robot must perform to maintain an internal representation of the environment. In addition, it can be very helpful for solving certain tasks in an efficient way, such as global navigation or self-localization.

2.1 Room modeling

Since rooms are assumed to be rectangular and its walls perpendicular to the floor, the problem of modeling a room from a set of regions can be treated as a rectangle detection problem. Several rectangle detection techniques can be found in the literature (Lagunovsky & Ablameyko, 1999; Lin & Nevatia, 1998; Tao et al., 2002). Most of them are based on a search in the 2D point space (for instance, a search in the edge representation of an image) using line primitives. These methods are computationally expensive and can be very sensitive to noisy data. In order to solve the modeling problem in an efficient way, we propose a new rectangle detection technique based on a search in the parameter space using a variation of the Hough Transform (Duda & Hart, 1972; Rosenfeld, 1969).

For line detection, several variations of the Hough Transform have been proposed (Matas et al., 2000; Palmer et al., 1994). The extension of the Hough Transform for rectangle detection is not new. (Zhu et al., 2003) proposes a *Rectangular Hough Transform* used to detect the center and orientation of a rectangle with known dimensions. (Jung & Schramm, 2004) proposes a *Windowed Hough Transform* that consists of searching rectangle patterns in the Hough space of every window of suitable dimensions of an image.

Our approach for rectangle detection uses a 3D version of the Hough Transform that facilitates the detection of segments instead of lines. This allows considering only those points that belong to the contour of a rectangle in the detection process. The Hough space is parameterized by (θ, d, p), being θ and d the parameters of the line representation ($d = x\cos(\theta) + y\sin(\theta)$) and $|p|$ the length of a segment in the line. For computing p it is assumed that one of the extreme points of its associated segment is initially fixed and situated at a distance of 0 to the perpendicular line passing through the origin. Under this assumption, being (x, y) the other extreme point of the segment, its *signed* length p can be computed as:

$$p = x\cos(\theta + \pi/2) + y\sin(\theta + \pi/2) \tag{1}$$

Using this representation, any point (x, y) contributes to those points (θ, d, p) in the Hough space that verifies:

$$d = x\cos(\theta) + y\sin(\theta) \tag{2}$$

and

$$p >= x\cos(\theta + \pi/2) + y\sin(\theta + \pi/2) \tag{3}$$

Equation 2 represents every line intersecting the point as in the original Hough Transform. The additional condition expressed by equation 3 limits the point contribution to those line segments containing the point. This allows computing the total number of points included in a given segment. For instance, given a segment with extreme points $V_i = (x_i, y_i)$ and $V_j = (x_j, y_j)$ and being H the 3D Hough space, the number of points that belong to the segment, which is denoted as $H_{i \leftrightarrow j}$, can be computed as:

$$H_{i \leftrightarrow j} = |H(\theta_{i \leftrightarrow j}, d_{i \leftrightarrow j}, p_i) - H(\theta_{i \leftrightarrow j}, d_{i \leftrightarrow j}, p_j)| \tag{4}$$

where $\theta_{i \leftrightarrow j}$ and $d_{i \leftrightarrow j}$ are the parameters of the common line to both points and p_i and p_j the *signed* lengths of the two segments with non-fixed extreme points V_i and V_j, respectively, according to equation 1.

Since a rectangle is composed by four segments, the 3D Hough space parameterized by (θ, d, p) allows computing the total number of points included in the contour of the rectangle. Thus, considering a rectangle expressed by its four vertices $V_1 = (x_1, y_1)$, $V_2 = (x_2, y_2)$, $V_3 = (x_3, y_3)$

and $V_4 = (x_4, y_4)$ (see figure 1), the number of points of its contour, denoted as H_r, can be computed as:

$$H_r = H_{1\leftrightarrow 2} + H_{2\leftrightarrow 3} + H_{3\leftrightarrow 4} + H_{4\leftrightarrow 1} \tag{5}$$

Considering the restrictions about the segments of the rectangle and using the equation 4, each $H_{i\leftrightarrow j}$ of the expression 5 can be rewritten as follows:

$$H_{1\leftrightarrow 2} = |H(\alpha, d_{1\leftrightarrow 2}, d_{4\leftrightarrow 1}) - H(\alpha, d_{1\leftrightarrow 2}, d_{2\leftrightarrow 3})| \tag{6}$$

$$H_{2\leftrightarrow 3} = |H(\alpha + \pi/2, d_{2\leftrightarrow 3}, d_{1\leftrightarrow 2}) - H(\alpha + \pi/2, d_{2\leftrightarrow 3}, d_{3\leftrightarrow 4})| \tag{7}$$

$$H_{3\leftrightarrow 4} = |H(\alpha, d_{3\leftrightarrow 4}, d_{2\leftrightarrow 3}) - H(\alpha, d_{3\leftrightarrow 4}, d_{4\leftrightarrow 1})| \tag{8}$$

$$H_{4\leftrightarrow 1} = |H(\alpha + \pi/2, d_{4\leftrightarrow 1}, d_{3\leftrightarrow 4}) - H(\alpha + \pi/2, d_{4\leftrightarrow 1}, d_{1\leftrightarrow 2})| \tag{9}$$

being α the orientation of the rectangle as expressed in figure 1 and $d_{i\leftrightarrow j}$ the normal distance of the origin to the straight line defined by the points V_i and V_j.
Since H_r expresses the number of points in a rectangle r defined by $(\alpha, d_{1\leftrightarrow 2}, d_{2\leftrightarrow 3}, d_{3\leftrightarrow 4}, d_{4\leftrightarrow 1})$, the problem of obtaining the best rectangle given a set of points can be solved by finding the combination of $(\alpha, d_{1\leftrightarrow 2}, d_{2\leftrightarrow 3}, d_{3\leftrightarrow 4}, d_{4\leftrightarrow 1})$ that maximizes H_r. This parametrization of the rectangle can be transformed into a more practical representation defined by the five-tuple (α, x_c, y_c, w, h), being (x_c, y_c) the central point of the rectangle and w and h its dimensions. This transformation can be achieved using the following expressions:

$$x_c = \frac{d_{1\leftrightarrow 2} + d_{3\leftrightarrow 4}}{2}\cos(\alpha) - \frac{d_{2\leftrightarrow 3} + d_{4\leftrightarrow 1}}{2}\sin(\alpha) \tag{10}$$

$$y_c = \frac{d_{1\leftrightarrow 2} + d_{3\leftrightarrow 4}}{2}\sin(\alpha) + \frac{d_{2\leftrightarrow 3} + d_{4\leftrightarrow 1}}{2}\cos(\alpha) \tag{11}$$

$$w = d_{2\leftrightarrow 3} - d_{4\leftrightarrow 1} \tag{12}$$

$$h = d_{3\leftrightarrow 4} - d_{1\leftrightarrow 2} \tag{13}$$

In order to compute H_r, the parameter space H is discretized assuming the rank $[-\pi/2, \pi/2]$ for θ and $[d_{min}, d_{max}]$ for d and p, being d_{min} and d_{max} the minimum and maximum distance, respectively, between a line and the origin. The sampling step of each parameter is chosen according to the required accuracy. Figure 1 shows an example of rectangle representation in the discretized parameter space. Each pair of parallel segments of the rectangle is represented in the corresponding orientation plane of the discrete Hough space: $H(\alpha_d)$ for one pair of segments and $H((\alpha + \pi/2)_d)$ for the other one, being α_d and $(\alpha + \pi/2)_d$ the discrete values associated to α (the rectangle orientation) and $(\alpha + \pi/2)$, respectively. For each orientation plane, it is represented how many points contribute to each cell (d_d, p_d), i.e. how many points belong to every segment of the corresponding orientation. A high histogram contribution is represented in the figure with a dark gray level, while a low contribution is depicted with an almost white color. As it can be observed, the maximum contributions are found in parallel segments with displacements of w_d and h_d, which are the discrete values associated to the rectangle dimensions.

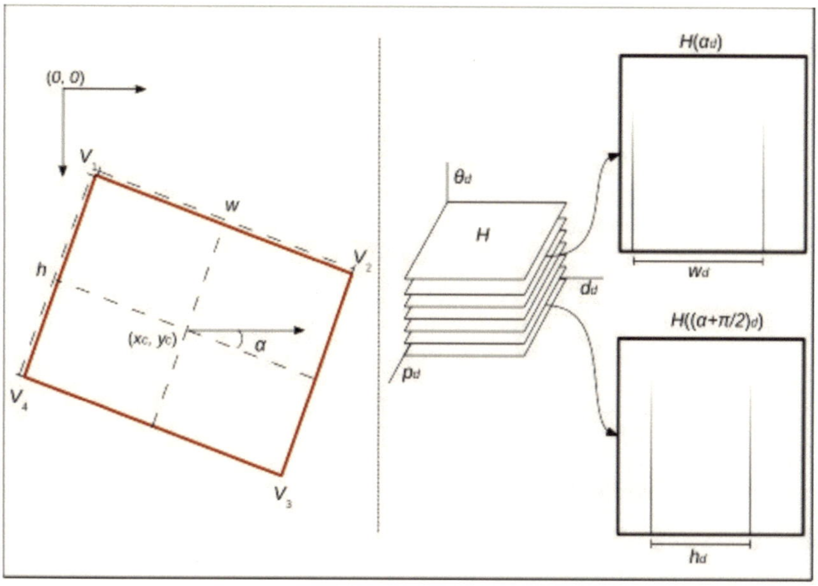

Fig. 1. Rectangle detection using the proposed 3D variation of the Hough Transform (see the text for further explanation)

This rectangle detection technique is used to obtain a room model that fits the points stored in the 3D occupancy grid. Walls are considered to have a maximum height and, therefore, only points situated at a certain rank of height in the grid are used for detecting the model. Assuming that this rank is in the interval $[0, Z_{wall}]$ and being G the 3D occupancy grid and τ the minimum occupancy value to considered a non empty region of the environment, the proposed method for room modeling can be summarized in the following steps:

1. Initialize all the cells of the discrete Hough space H to 0.
2. For each cell, $G(x_d, y_d, z_d)$, such that $G(x_d, y_d, z_d).occupancy > \tau$ and $z_d \epsilon [0, Z_{wall}]$:

   Compute the real coordinates (x, y) associated to the cell indexes (x_d, y_d).

   For $\theta_d = \theta_{dMin} \ldots \theta_{dMax}$:
   (a) Compute the real value θ associated to θ_d.
   (b) Compute $d = x\cos(\theta) + y\sin(\theta)$.
   (c) Compute the discrete value d_d associated to d.
   (d) Compute $p = x\cos(\theta + \pi/2) + y\sin(\theta + \pi/2)$.
   (e) Compute the discrete value p_d associated to p.
   (f) For $p'_d = p_d \ldots d_{dMax}$: increment $H(\theta_d, d_d, p'_d)$ by 1.
3. Compute $\underset{\alpha, d_{1\leftrightarrow 2}, d_{2\leftrightarrow 3}, d_{3\leftrightarrow 4}, d_{4\leftrightarrow 1}}{\arg\max} H_r(\alpha, d_{1\leftrightarrow 2}, d_{2\leftrightarrow 3}, d_{3\leftrightarrow 4}, d_{4\leftrightarrow 1})$.
4. Obtain the rectangle $r = (\alpha, x_c, y_c, w, h)$ using equations 10, 11, 12 and 13.

2.2 Door detection

Doors are free passage zones that connect two different rooms, so they can be considered as empty segments of the corresponding room rectangle (i.e. segments without points). Taking this into account, once the room model is obtained, doors can be detected by analyzing each wall segment in the 3D Hough space. Thus, for each segment of the rectangle defined by V_i and V_j, two points $D_k = (x_k, y_k)$ and $D_l = (x_l, y_l)$ situated on the inside of that segment constitutes a door segment if it is verified:

$$H_{k \leftrightarrow l} = |H(\theta_{i \leftrightarrow j}, d_{i \leftrightarrow j}, p_k) - H(\theta_{i \leftrightarrow j}, d_{i \leftrightarrow j}, p_l)| = 0 \quad (14)$$

being $\theta_{i \leftrightarrow j}$ and $d_{i \leftrightarrow j}$ the parameters of the straight line defined by V_i and V_j and p_k and p_l the *signed* lengths of the segments for D_k and D_l:

$$p_k = x_k \cos(\theta_{i \leftrightarrow j} + \pi/2) + y_k \sin(\theta_{i \leftrightarrow j} + \pi/2) \quad (15)$$

$$p_l = x_l \cos(\theta_{i \leftrightarrow j} + \pi/2) + y_l \sin(\theta_{i \leftrightarrow j} + \pi/2) \quad (16)$$

Assuming $p_i \leq p_k < p_l \leq p_j$ and a minimum length l for each door segment, the door detection process can be carried out by verifying equation 14 for every pair of points between V_i and V_j, such that $p_l - p_k \geq l$. Starting from the discrete representation of the Hough space, this process can be summarized in the following steps:

1. Compute the discrete value θ_d associated to θ_{i-j}.
2. Compute the discrete value d_d associated to d_{i-j}.
3. Compute the discrete value p_{di} associated to p_i.
4. Compute the discrete value p_{dj} associated to p_j.
5. Compute the discrete value l_d associated to l (minimum length of doors).
6. $p_{dk} \leftarrow p_{di}$
7. While $p_{dk} \leq p_{dj} - l_d$:
   (a) $p_{dl} \leftarrow p_{dk} + 1$
   (b) While $p_{dl} < p_{dj}$ and $|H(\theta_d, d_d, p_{dk}) - H(\theta_d, d_d, p_{dl})| = 0$: $p_{dl} \leftarrow p_{dl} + 1$
   (c) If $p_{dl} - p_{dk} > l_d$:
      i. Compute the real value p_k associated to p_{dk}.
      ii. Compute the real value p_l associated to $(p_{dl} - 1)$.
      iii. Compute the door limits D_k and D_l from p_k and p_l.
      iv. Insert the new door segment with extreme points D_k and D_l to the list of doors.
   (d) $p_{dk} \leftarrow p_{dl}$

The output of this method is the list of doors of the wall segment delimited by the vertices V_i and V_j. Each door is represented by its extreme points D_k and D_l, which are computed in step 7.(c).iii. from p_k and p_l. Since both points verify the line equation ($d_{i \leftrightarrow j} = x \cos(\theta_{i \leftrightarrow j}) + y \sin(\theta_{i \leftrightarrow j})$), using 15 and 16, their coordinates can be computed as follows:

$$x_k = d_{i \leftrightarrow j} \cos(\theta_{i \leftrightarrow j}) - p_k \sin(\theta_{i \leftrightarrow j}) \quad (17)$$

$$y_k = d_{i \leftrightarrow j} \sin(\theta_{i \leftrightarrow j}) + p_k \cos(\theta_{i \leftrightarrow j}) \quad (18)$$

$$x_l = d_{i \leftrightarrow j} \cos(\theta_{i \leftrightarrow j}) - p_l \sin(\theta_{i \leftrightarrow j}) \quad (19)$$

$$y_l = d_{i \leftrightarrow j} \sin(\theta_{i \leftrightarrow j}) + p_l \cos(\theta_{i \leftrightarrow j}) \quad (20)$$

2.3 Topological and metric representation of the environment

The detected rooms and doors are modeled and used to build a topological representation of the environment. In this representation, the environment is described as an undirected graph whose vertices represent the different explored rooms (see figure 2). An edge linking two vertices expresses the existence of a door that connects two rooms. This is a very useful representation for the robot to effectively move around man-made environments. For instance, the robot could analyze the graph to obtain the minimum path connecting any two rooms. Moreover, this representation can be extended using recursive descriptions to express more complex world structures like buildings. Thus, a building could be represented by a node containing several interconnected subgraphs. Each subgraph would represent a floor of the building and contain a description of the interconnections between the different rooms and corridors in it.

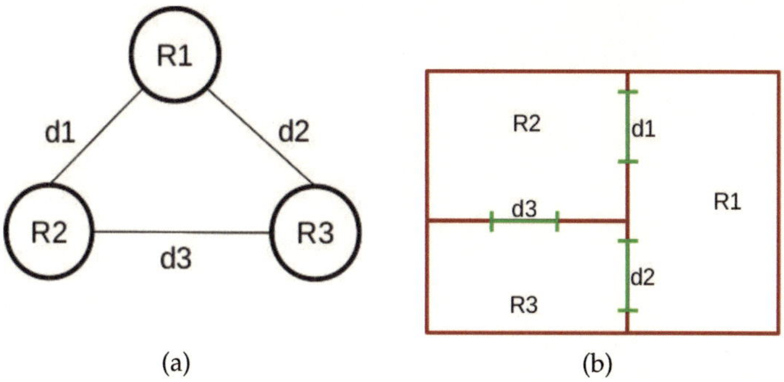

Fig. 2. Topological representation (a) of an environment (b) composed by three intercommunicated rooms.

Using this topological graph, a minimal set of metric information is maintained. Specifically, each vertex of the graph stores the parametric description of the corresponding room and its doors. Metric maps of the environment can be easily computed from this representation when necessary (e.g. when the robot has to compute a metric path connecting two rooms). In order to maintain this basic metric representation, each room model contains a reference frame (F_r) which expresses the location of the room in relation to a global reference frame (F_w). The room reference frame is located at the room center with a rotation given by the room orientation. Thus, being $r = (\alpha, x_c, y_c, w, h)$ the rectangle that models a given room, the transformation matrix (T_r) that relates F_r with F_w is defined as:

$$T_r = \begin{pmatrix} \cos(\alpha) & -\sin(\alpha) & 0 & x_c \\ \sin(\alpha) & \cos(\alpha) & 0 & y_c \\ 0 & 0 & 1 & 0 \\ 0 & 0 & 0 & 1 \end{pmatrix} \tag{21}$$

This matrix provides the transformation $p_w = T_r p_r$, being p_w and p_r the homogeneous coordinates of a 3D point viewed from F_w and F_r, respectively. In the same way, the coordinates of a point in a room $r1$ can be transformed into coordinates expressed in other room ($r2$) reference frame by applying the corresponding sequence of transformations:

$$p_{r2} = T_{r2}^{-1} T_{r1} p_{r1} \tag{22}$$

where p_{r1} is a point situated inside the room $r1$, p_{r2} is the same point viewed from the reference frame of the room $r2$ and T_{r1} and T_{r2} are the transformation matrices of the reference frames of $r1$ and $r2$, respectively.
If two rooms, $r1$ and $r2$, are communicated by a door, points of the door are common to both rooms. Assume a door point d_{r1} viewed from the room $r1$ and the corresponding point d_{r2} of the room $r2$. The metric representation of both rooms would ideally be subject to the following restriction:

$$\|T_{r2}d_{r2} - T_{r1}d_{r1}\|^2 = 0 \tag{23}$$

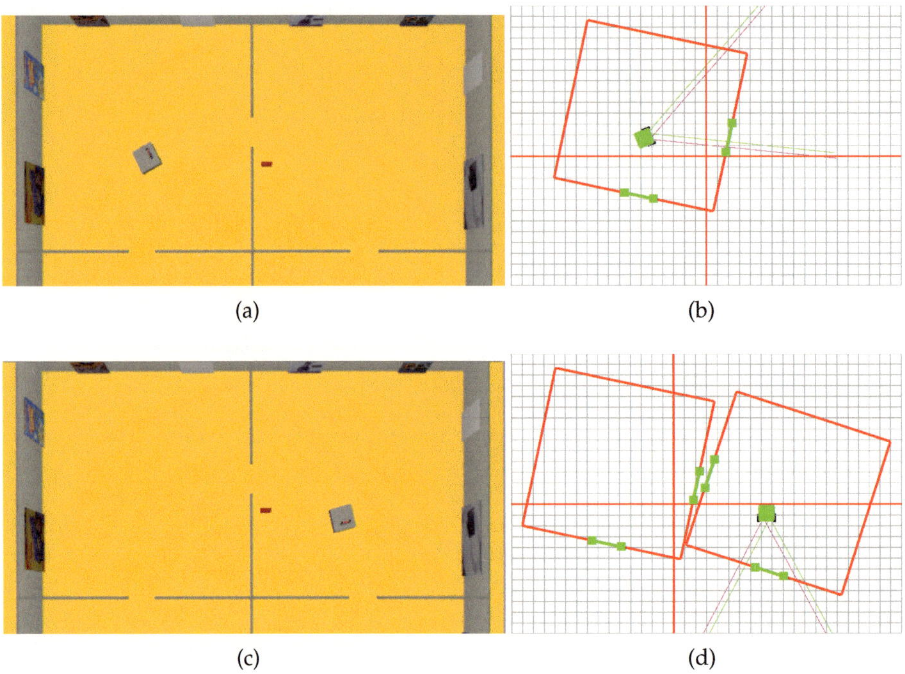

Fig. 3. Deviation between the position of a door common to two rooms caused by odometric errors (results obtained using the gazebo simulator): (a) overhead view of the scene after the creation of the first room model; (b) metric representation of the first room; (c) overhead view of the scene after the creation of the second room model, (d) metric representation of the two rooms.

During exploration, odometric errors cause deviations between the positions of a common door to two adjacent rooms and therefore expression 23 is usually not verified when a new room model is created (see figure 3). However, these deviations allow computing how the reference frame of each room model should be modified in order to fulfill with the *common door restriction*. Thus, given $d^{(1)}$ and $d^{(2)}$, extreme points of the common door, the rotational and translational deviations ($\triangle\alpha$ and $\triangle t$) between two adjacent room models can be computed as:

$$\triangle\alpha = \arctan\left(\frac{y_{r2}^{(1)} - y_{r2}^{(2)}}{x_{r2}^{(1)} - x_{r2}^{(2)}}\right) - \arctan\left(\frac{y_{r1}^{(1)} - y_{r1}^{(2)}}{x_{r1}^{(1)} - x_{r1}^{(2)}}\right) \tag{24}$$

$$\triangle t = d_{r2}^{(1)} - \begin{pmatrix} \cos(\triangle\alpha) & -\sin(\triangle\alpha) & 0 \\ \sin(\triangle\alpha) & \cos(\triangle\alpha) & 0 \\ 0 & 0 & 1 \end{pmatrix} d_{r1}^{(1)} \tag{25}$$

being $d_{rj}^{(i)} = (x_{rj}^{(i)}, y_{rj}^{(i)}, z_{rj}^{(i)})^T$ the door point $d^{(i)}$ expressed in the reference frame of the model rj.

Assuming an egocentric metric system, the robot pose and the reference frame of the current room model are not affected by these deviations. This implies that remaining room models must be moved according to equations 24 and 25. Thus, for every room model $ri = (\alpha_i, x_{ci}, y_{ci}, w_i, h_i)$ different than the current one, its reference frame is updated as follows:

$$\alpha_i \leftarrow \alpha_i + \triangle\alpha \tag{26}$$

$$\begin{pmatrix} x_{ci} \\ y_{ci} \\ 0 \end{pmatrix} \leftarrow \begin{pmatrix} \cos(\triangle\alpha) & -\sin(\triangle\alpha) & 0 \\ \sin(\triangle\alpha) & \cos(\triangle\alpha) & 0 \\ 0 & 0 & 1 \end{pmatrix} \begin{pmatrix} x_{ci} \\ y_{ci} \\ 0 \end{pmatrix} + \triangle t \tag{27}$$

Figure 4 shows the result of applying this correction to the metric representation of figure 3. In case of using an eccentric representation, the robot pose and the reference frame of the current model are corrected applying the deviations $\triangle\alpha$ and $\triangle t$ in inverse order.

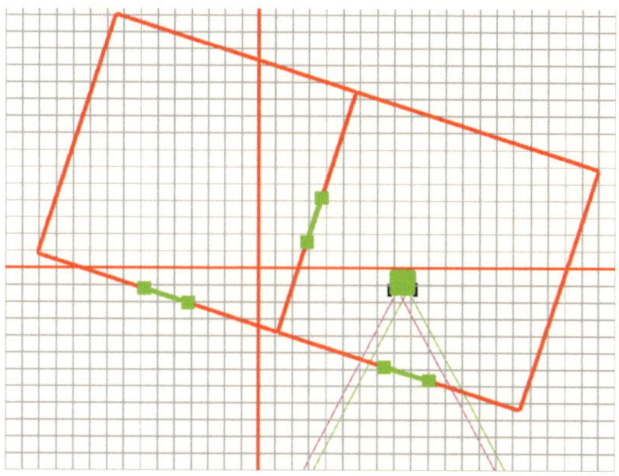

Fig. 4. Metric correction of the environment representation of figure 3 based on the common door restriction.

A similar correction must be carried out to deal with odometric errors when the robot is in a previously modeled room. In such cases, the pose of the robot relative to the room where it is located can be computed according to the new location of the room. To estimate the new location, perceived regions must be used to detect a room model with known dimensions following the detection process of section 2.1. Being $r(i) = (\alpha(i), x_c(i), y_c(i), w, h)$ the room model at instant i and $r(i+1) = (\alpha(i+1), x_c(i+1), y_c(i+1), w, h)$ a new estimation of the room model at $i+1$, the model deviation can be computed as:

$$\triangle\alpha = \alpha(i+1) - \alpha(i) \tag{28}$$

$$\triangle t = \begin{pmatrix} x_c(i+1) \\ y_c(i+1) \\ 0 \end{pmatrix} - \begin{pmatrix} \cos(\triangle\alpha) & -\sin(\triangle\alpha) & 0 \\ \sin(\triangle\alpha) & \cos(\triangle\alpha) & 0 \\ 0 & 0 & 1 \end{pmatrix} \begin{pmatrix} x_c(i) \\ y_c(i) \\ 0 \end{pmatrix} \tag{29}$$

Using these equations, the robot pose in an eccentric representation or the reference frames of room models in an egocentric one are corrected. Figure 5 shows an example. This correction is only applied when there exists no ambiguity in the result of the new estimation of the room model. This means that if the set of perceived regions can be associated to more than one model, the new estimation is rejected.

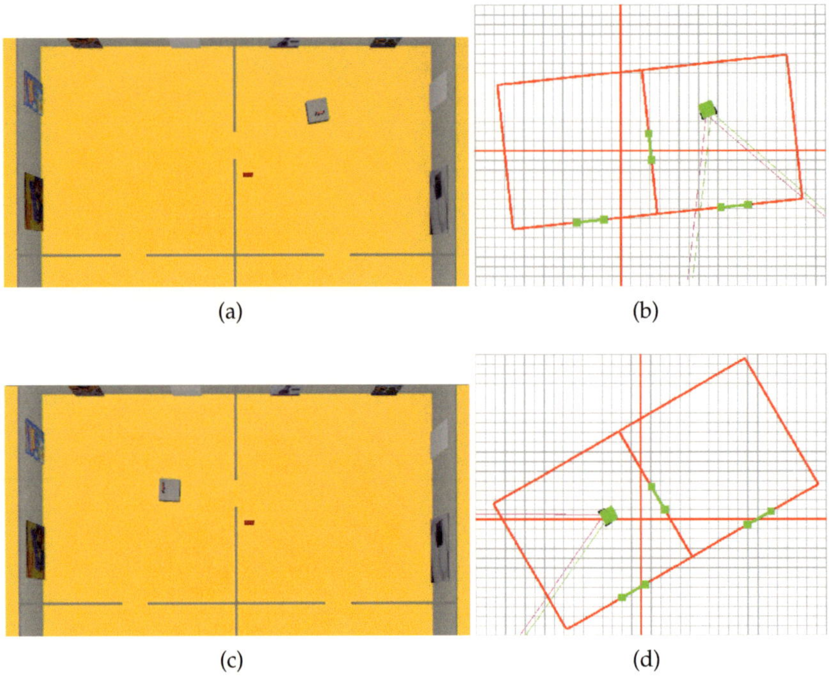

(a) (b) (c) (d)

Fig. 5. Metric correction through room model re-estimation.

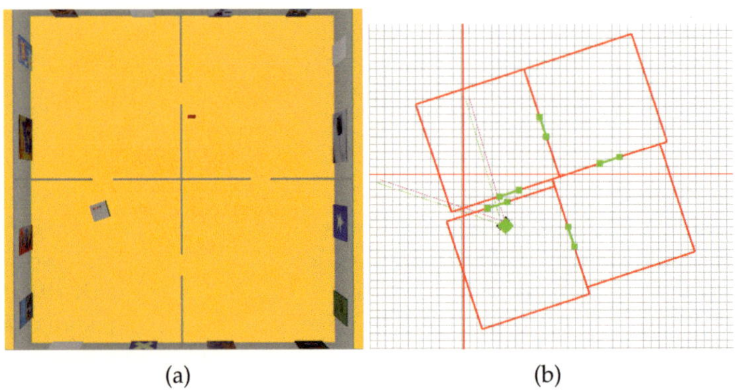

(a) (b)

Fig. 6. Metric errors in a loop closing.

Another critical problem to take into account in the creation of a metric representation of the environment are loop closings. The term *loop closing* refers to the return to a previously visited place after an exploration of arbitrary length. These situations occur when the robot detects a new door which is connected to a previously visited room. In such cases, new corrections must be done to minimize the error in the position of the detected common door (see figure 6). However, this error is caused by an imperfect estimation of the parameters of rooms and doors and, therefore, a unique correction will surely not solve the problem. A solution to this problem is to distribute the parameter adjustment among every model in the metric representation (Olson, 2008). The basic idea of this approach is to minimize a global error function defined over the whole metric representation by introducing small variations in the different elements composing that representation. These variations are constrained by the uncertainty of the measurement, so *high-confident* parameters remain almost unchanged during the error minimization process.

In our environment representation, the global error is defined in terms of deviations between the positions of the doors connecting adjacent rooms. Thus, the error function to minimize can be expressed as:

$$\xi = \sum_{\forall connected(d_{ri}^{(n)}, d_{rj}^{(m)})} \| T_{ri} d_{ri}^{(n)} - T_{rj} d_{rj}^{(m)} \|^2 \tag{30}$$

being $d_{ri}^{(n)}$ and $d_{rj}^{(m)}$ the middle points of a common door expressed in the reference frames of rooms ri and rj, respectively, and T_{ri} and T_{rj} the transformation matrices of such rooms.

To minimize ξ, we use the Stochastic Gradient Descent (Robbins & Monro, 1951), which has proven to be an efficient method to solve similar problems (Olson, 2008). In SGD, the error function is iteratively reduced by randomly selecting a parameter and modifying it using a gradient descent step. Each step is modulated by a *learning rate* λ which is reduced over time to avoid local minima. Being S the set of parameters and ξ the error function, the method proceeds as follows:

1. Initialize λ
2. While not converge:
   (a) randomly select a parameter s_i of the set S
   (b) Compute the step of s_i ($\triangle s_i$) in the gradient descent direction of ξ according to the uncertainty of s_i.
   (c) Modify s_i: $s_i \leftarrow s_i + \lambda \triangle s_i$
   (d) Update λ: $\lambda \leftarrow \lambda / (\lambda + 1)$

The set of parameters affecting the error function of equation 30 are those related to room and door models. In door models, the only parameter susceptible to variations is its central position relative to the corresponding wall. Assuming the order of walls in figure 7(a), this position ($c_{rk}^{(l)}$) corresponds to the first coordinate for doors in walls 1 and 3 or to the second one for doors in walls 2 and 4. Thus, an adjustment of a door position $d_{rk}^{(l)}$ through a variation $\triangle c_{rk}^{(l)}$ can be written as:

$$d_{rk}^{(l)} \leftarrow (c_{rk}^{(l)} + \triangle c_{rk}^{(l)}, -h_{rk}/2, 0)^T \quad for\ doors\ in\ wall\ 1 \tag{31}$$

$$d_{rk}^{(l)} \leftarrow (w_{rk}/2, c_{rk}^{(l)} + \triangle c_{rk}^{(l)}, 0)^T \quad for\ doors\ in\ wall\ 2 \tag{32}$$

$$d_{rk}^{(l)} \leftarrow (c_{rk}^{(l)} + \triangle c_{rk}^{(l)}, h_{rk}/2, 0)^T \quad for\ doors\ in\ wall\ 3 \tag{33}$$

$$d_{rk}^{(l)} \leftarrow (-w_{rk}/2, c_{rk}^{(l)} + \triangle c_{rk}^{(l)}, 0)^T \quad for\ doors\ in\ wall\ 4 \tag{34}$$

being h_{rk} and w_{rk} the height and width of the room rk.
Regarding room parameters, potential errors in the detection process may affect only to the estimation of the room dimensions (h_{rk} and w_{rk}). Thus, any variation in a room model should be associated to these parameters. However, since every wall corresponds to a segment of the room model and the uncertainty in the detection process is associated to segments and not to model dimensions, the position of every wall is individually adjusted (see 7(b)). These wall adjustments modify the dimensions of the rooms as follows:

$$h_{rk} \leftarrow h_{rk} + \triangle h_{rk}^{(2)} - \triangle h_{rk}^{(1)} \tag{35}$$

$$w_{rk} \leftarrow w_{rk} + \triangle w_{rk}^{(2)} - \triangle w_{rk}^{(1)} \tag{36}$$

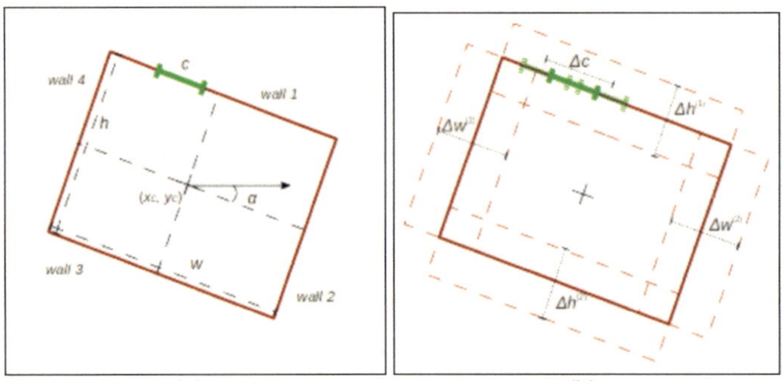

(a) (b)

Fig. 7. 7(a) Parametrization of room and door models ; 7(b) Adjustable parameters of rooms and doors.

In addition, changes in wall positions can modify the center of the model. Therefore, for any change in a wall position, the room transformation matrix must be updated as follows:

$$T_{rk} \leftarrow T_{rk} \begin{pmatrix} 1\,0\,0 & (\triangle w_{rk}^{(1)} + \triangle w_{rk}^{(2)})/2 \\ 0\,1\,0 & (\triangle h_{rk}^{(1)} + \triangle h_{rk}^{(2)})/2 \\ 0\,0\,1 & 0 \\ 0\,0\,0 & 1 \end{pmatrix} \tag{37}$$

Thus, using the set of parameters formed by each door central position ($c_{rk}^{(l)}$) and each room wall position ($h_{rk}^{(1)}, h_{rk}^{(2)}, w_{rk}^{(1)}, w_{rk}^{(2)}$), the error function ξ of equation 30 is minimized following the SGD method previously described. It must be taken into account that when the selected parameter is a wall position the transformation matrix of the corresponding room must be updated according to equation 37. Figure 8 shows the result of applying this method to the metric representation of figure 6.

3. The attention-based control architecture

As it was stated in the introduction of this chapter, in order to provide the robot with the ability to explore and model its environment in an autonomous way, it is necessary to endow it with different perceptual behaviors. Perception should be strongly linked to the robot actions in such a way that deciding where to look is influenced by what the robot is doing and also

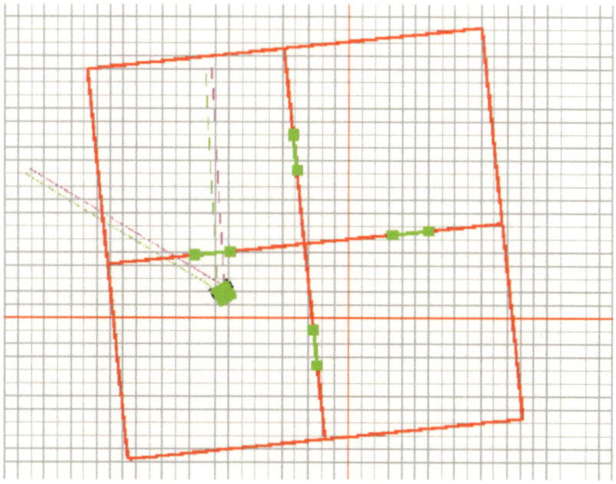

Fig. 8. Metric correction of the loop closing errors of figure 6.

in a way that the actions of the robot are limited by what is being perceived. These double link between perception and action is solved using the attention-based control architecture (Bachiller et al., 2008).

The proposed attention-based control architecture is composed by three intercommunicated subsystems: the behavioral system, the visual attention system and the motor control system. The behavioral system generates high-level actions that allows keeping different behavioral objectives in the robot. The visual attention system contains the ocular fixation mechanisms that provide the selection and foveatization of visual targets. These two systems are connected to the motor control system, which is responsible of executing the motor responses generated by both of them.

Each high-level behavior modulates the visual attention system in an specific way to get the most suitable flow of visual information according to its behavioral goals. At every execution cycle, the attention system selects a single visual target and sends it to the behavioral system, which executes the most appropriate action according to the received visual information. Thus, the attention system also modulates the behavioral one. This double modulation (from the behavioral system to the attention system and from the attention system to the behavioral one) endows the robot with both deliberative and reactive abilities since it can drive the perceptual process according to the needs or intentions of the robot, but its actions are conditioned by the outside world. This makes the robot interact in an effective way with a real and non-structured environment.

3.1 Attentional requirements

The function of attention in our system is strongly linked to the selection for action mechanisms (Allport, 1987), since it is used to select the most suitable stimulus for action execution. From this point of view, the attention system should maintain the following performance requirements: a) the selection of a visual target should be conditioned by its visual properties; b) this selection should also be influenced by the behavioral intentions or necessities of the robot; c) the system must provide a single focus of attention acting as the only visual input of every high-level behavior; d) the system should be able to simultaneously maintain several visual targets in order to alternate among them covering this way the perceptual needs of every high-level behavior. All these requirements can be fulfilled combining four kinds of attention:

- Bottom-up attention

- Top-down attention
- Overt attention
- Covert attention

These modes of attention can be found at some degree in the different computational models proposed in the literature. Some of them employ a pure bottom-up strategy (Itti & Koch, 2000; Koch & Ullman, 1985), while others integrate contextual information (Torralba et al., 2006) or knowledge about relevant properties of the visual targets along with the sensory data (Frintrop, 2006; Navalpakkam & Itti, 2006). All of them provide overt or covert attention, since the result of the attentional process is the selection of the most salient or conspicuous visual region. If this selection implies eyes movements, it is called overt attention. If it only produces a mental focusing on the selected region, the attention is covert.

Despite the variety of proposals, all these models are characterized by a common aspect: attention control is centralized. It is to say, the result of every processing unit of the system in these models is used by an unique control component that is responsible for driving attention. The centralization of the attentional control presents some problems that prevent from solving key aspects of our proposal. These problems can be summarized in the following three points:

1. Specification of multiple targets
2. Attentional shifts among different targets
3. Reaction to unexpected stimuli

From the point of view of complex actions, the robot needs to maintain several behavioral goals which will be frequently guided by different visual targets. If attentional control is centralized, the specification of multiple visual targets could not work well because the system has to integrate all the selection criteria in an unique support (a saliency or conspicuity map) that represents the relevance of every visual region. This integration becomes complicated (or even unfeasible) when some aspects of one target are in contradiction with the specification of other target, leading sometimes to a wrong attentional behavior. Even though an effective integration of multiple targets could be achieved, another question remains: how to shift attention at the required frequency from one type of target to another one? In a centralized control system, mechanisms as inhibition of return do not solve this question, since the integration of multiple stimuli cancels the possibility of distinguishing among different kinds of targets. A potential solution to both problems could consist of dynamically modulating the visual system for attending only one kind of target at a time. This allows shifting attention among different visual regions at the desired frequency, avoiding any problem related to the integration of multiple targets. However, this solution presents an important weakness: attention can only be programmed to focus on expected things and so the robot could not be able to react to unforeseen stimuli.

In order to overcome these limitations, we propose a distributed system of visual attention, in which the selection of the focus of attention is accomplished by multiple control units called *attentional selectors*. Each attentional selector drives attention from different top-down specifications to focus on different types of visual targets. At any given time, overt attention is driven by one attentional selector, while the rest attends covertly to their corresponding targets. The frequency at which an attentional selector operates overtly is modulated by the high level behavioral units depending on its information requirements. This approach solves the problems described previously. Firstly, it admits the coexistence of different types of visual targets, providing a clearer and simpler design of the selection mechanisms than a centralized approach. Secondly, each attentional selector is modulated to focus attention on the corresponding target at a given frequency. This prevents from constantly centering attention on the same visual target and guarantees an appropriate distribution of the attention time among the different targets. Lastly, since several attentional selectors can operate simultaneously, covert attention on a visual region can be transformed into overt attention as soon as it is necessary, allowing the robot to appropriately react to any situation.

3.2 A distributed system of visual attention

The proposed visual attention system presents the general structure of figure 9. The perception components are related to image acquisition, detection of regions of interest (Harris-Laplace regions) and extraction of geometrical and appearance features of each detected region. These features are used by a set of components, called attentional selectors, to drive attention according to certain top-down behavioral specifications. Attentional control is not centralized, but distributed among several attentional selectors. Each of them makes its own selection process to focus on an specific type of visual region. For this purpose, they individually compute a saliency map that represents the relevancy of each region according to their top-down specifications. This saliency map acts as a control surface whose maxima match with candidate visual regions to get the focus of attention.

The simultaneous execution of multiple attentional selectors requires including an overt-attention controller that decides which individually selected region gains the overt focus of attention at each moment. Attentional selectors attend covertly to their selected regions. They request the overt-attention controller to take overt control of attention at a certain frequency that is modulated by high-level behavioral units. This frequency depends on the information requirements of the corresponding behavior, so, at any moment, several target selectors could try to get the overt control of attention. To deal with this situation, the overt-attention controller maintains a time stamp for each active attentional selector that indicates when to yield control to that individual selector. Every so often, the overt-attention controller analyses the time stamp of every attentional selector. The selector with the oldest mark is then chosen for driving the overt control of attention. If several selectors share the oldest time stamp, the one with the highest frequency acquires motor control. Frequencies of individual selectors can be interpreted as alerting levels that allow keeping a higher or lower attention degree on the corresponding target. This way, the described strategy gives priority to those selectors with the highest alerting level that require faster control responses.

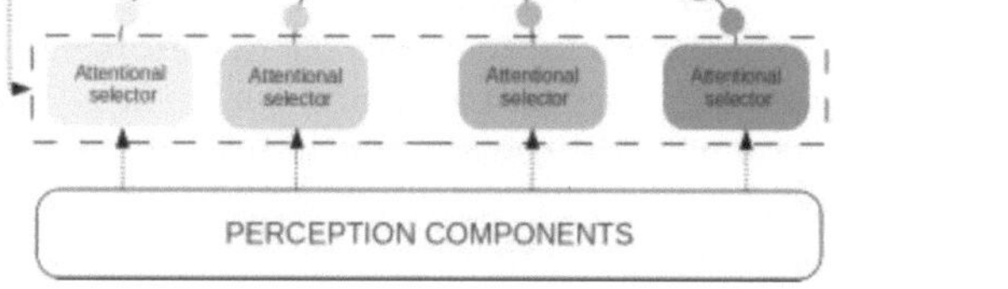

Fig. 9. General structure of the proposed distributed system of visual attention

Once the overt focus of attention is selected, it is sent to the high-level behavioral components. Only actions compatible with the focus of attention are then executed, providing a mechanism of coordination among behaviors. In addition, the selected visual region is centered in the images of the stereo pair, achieving a binocular overt fixation of the current target until another visual target is selected.

Our proposal for this binocular fixation is to use a cooperative control scheme in which each camera plays a different role in the global control. Thus, the 3D fixation movement is separated into two movements: a monocular tracking movement in one on the cameras (the dominant camera) and an asymmetric vergence movement in the other one (secondary camera). This separation allows the saccade that provides the initial fixation on the target to be programmed for a single camera while maintaining a stable focus in both cameras (Enright, 1998). In addition, this scheme provides an effective response to situations in which it is not possible to obtain a complete correspondence of the target in the pair of images due to the change of perspective, the partial occlusion in one of the views or even the non-visibility of the target from one of the cameras.

4. Active modeling using the attention-based control architecture

In an active modeling process, the robot must be able to explore and build a representation of the environment in an unsupervised way (i.e. without human intervention). The different perceptive and high-level behaviors taking part in this process have to deal with different issues: look for the walls of the room, detect obstacles in the path when the robot is moving, decide whether what appears to be door is an actual door or not, or decide when to start exploring another place of the environment, among others. To endow the robot with the required capability to solve all these questions, we propose the behavioral system of figure 10 which follows our attention based-control approach.

Each behavioral and attentional component of the proposed system has an specific role in the modeling task. The Active Modeler behavior starts the task by gaining access to the visual information around the robot. For this purpose, it activates an attentional selector, which attends to visual regions of interest situated in front of the robot, and starts turning the robot base around. The rotational velocity varies according to the attentional response in such a way that the speed increases if no visual region is perceived in front of the robot. Once the robot returns to its initial orientation, a first model of the room is obtained. This model is the rectangular configuration of walls that best fits the set of perceived regions. The resulting model is then improved by the Room Verifier behavior, which forces the robot to approach to those regions with higher uncertainty. To accomplish its goal, Room Verifier activates an attentional selector that changes the gaze so the cameras point towards those visual regions situated at high uncertainty zones. At the same time, it sends the goal positions to the Go to Point behavior in order to make the robot approach those zones. This last behavior is connected to an attentional selector of obstacles, which shifts attention towards regions situated close to the trajectory between the robot and the goal position. The Go to Point behavior interprets the incoming visual information as the nearest regions that could interfere in the approach to the destination position and generates changes in the robot trajectory according to this. In this situation, the focus of attention alternates between uncertainty regions and potential obstacles, keeping overt control on one of the targets and covert control on the other one. This behavior forces the robot to react appropriately to obstacles while the goal position can be quickly recovered and updated. Once the whole uncertainty of the model is low enough, it is considered stable and new behaviors take place. Specifically, the robot tries to locate untextured zones on the walls and hypothesizes them as potential doors that

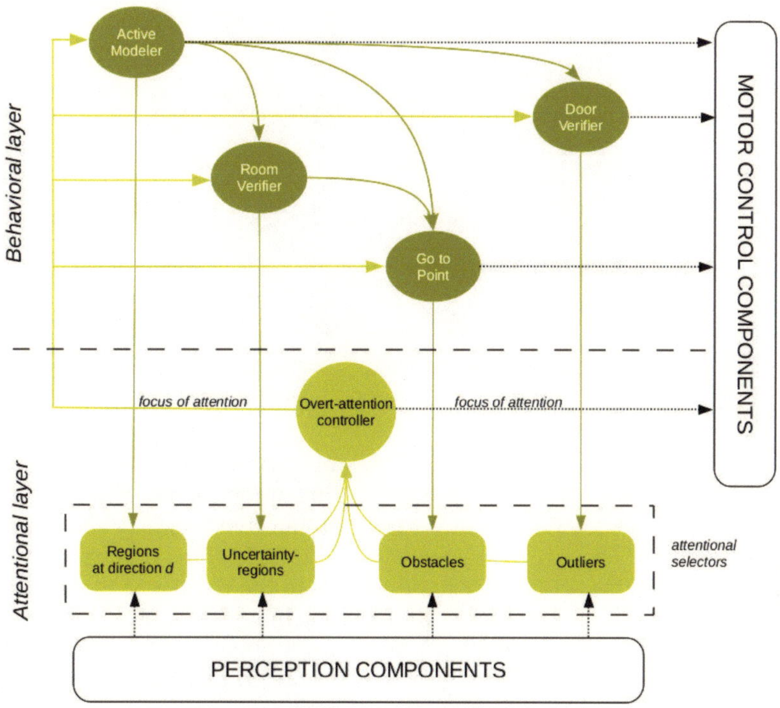

Fig. 10. Scheme of the proposed behavioral system for environment modeling

must be verified. At that time, the Active Modeler behavior reconfigures the corresponding attentional selector to focus on visual regions in the direction of the door where the robot has to approach. Once again, the approaching action is solved by the Go to Point component, taking advantages of the distributed attentional control. When the robot is near enough a potential door, the Door Verifier behavior tries to verify the current hypothesis searching for regions situated behind the corresponding wall. To do so, it activates an attentional selector which selects regions that can be considered as outliers of the room model. If necessary, the Door Verifier behavior spins the base of the robot to cover the whole space of the door. Using the visual information that has been recovered during this process, the robot decides whether to reject or accept the door hypothesis as a real door. If accepted as a real door, the robot gets out of the room to explore unknown spaces driven by the Active Modeler behavior. The room left behind is reduced to a minimal geometric parametrization and stored as a node in the graph representing the topological space. Finally, the whole process is re-initiated and new models are obtained, giving rise over time to a complete topological representation of the environment.

5. Experimental results

We have carried out different experiments in real indoor environments. They were designed to demonstrate the modeling ability of a mobile robot equipped with a stereo vision head. In particular, we used RobEx (figure 11), an open-hardware robotic platform. For the experiments, RobEx was equipped with a 4-dof stereo vision head providing: a neck-movement followed by a common tilt and two independent camera pan movements (Mateos et al., 2010).

Fig. 11. The RobEx platform.

In the first experiment, we tested the ability of the robot to model a room with several objects on the floor. Figure 12 shows the result of this experiment for the modeling of the room at the right side of figure 13. Figure 12(a) shows the set of perceived regions after an autonomous exploration of the room. These regions are associated to cells of the occupancy grid with high certainty degree. From this set of points, the models of the room and the door are detected (figure 12(b)). The metric representation of the resulting models is shown in figure 12(c). Using this room model, the occupancy grid is updated to cover only the local space inside the room. In addition, the positions of the points near to walls are adjusted according to the detected model. Figure 12(d) shows the result of this adjustment.

In the second experiment, the robot modeled an environment composed by two rooms communicated by a door (figure 14). Figures 15 and 16 show the evolution of the modeling process during the environment exploration. Specifically, for the modeling of the first room, the results of the robot behavior can be observed in figures 15(a) to 15(d): (a) an initial model is created fixating attention on frontal visual regions while the robot base turns around; (b) the robot verifies the room model by keeping attention on high uncertainty zones while approaching them. This allows correcting the model parameters as well as discarding the false door on the right of figure (a); (c) the door is verified and its parameters are adjusted by fixating attention on regions situated outside of the room; (d) the robot gets out of the room to start exploring the second room. Once the robot gets into the new room, the modeling process is repeated for detecting a new model as it is shown in figures 16(a) to 16(c): (a) initial model creation; (b) room model verifying stage; (c) door verifying stage. Finally (figure 16(d)) the deviation between the two room models is corrected applying the common door restriction.

The last experiment tested the ability of the robot to model a more complex configuration of the environment. The environment of the experiment was composed by three intercommunicated rooms with different dimensions (figure 18). Figure 17 shows the modeling results during the exploration of each room. After creating the final model of every room, the deviation of the new model is corrected according to the door connecting the room to an existing model. Finally, it is obtained an environment representation that corresponds to a great extent with the real scene. The error in the dimensions of the first room (see figure 17(e)) is due to the discretization of the Hough space. This kind of errors are considered in the representation of the model as part of its uncertainty. It is important to note that this uncertainty is local to the model. Thus, as it is shown in figure 17, there is no error propagation in the creation of remaining models composing the final representation of the environment.

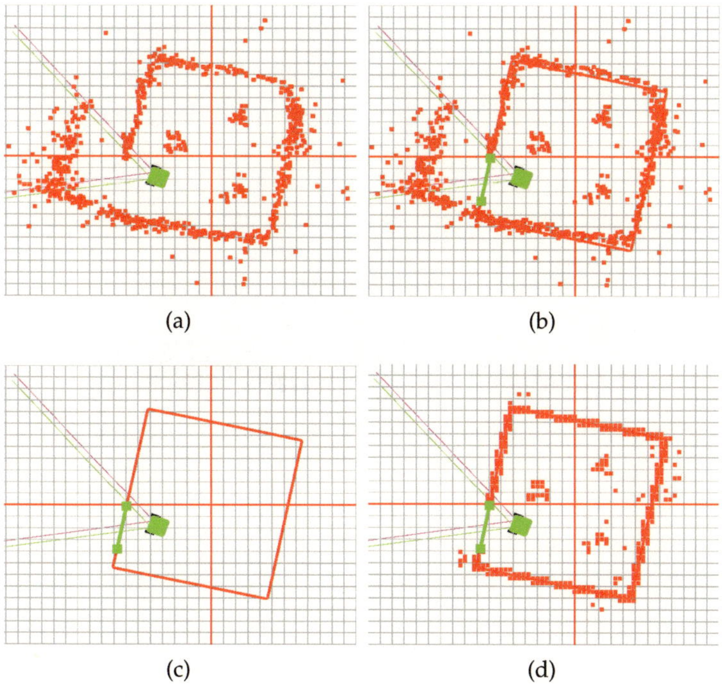

Fig. 12. Room modeling process: (a) 2D view of the perceived regions during the exploration; (b) room and door models detection from the set of points in (a); (c) metric representation of the room; (d) state of the occupancy grid after fixating the room model in (c). These results correspond to the environment shown in 13.

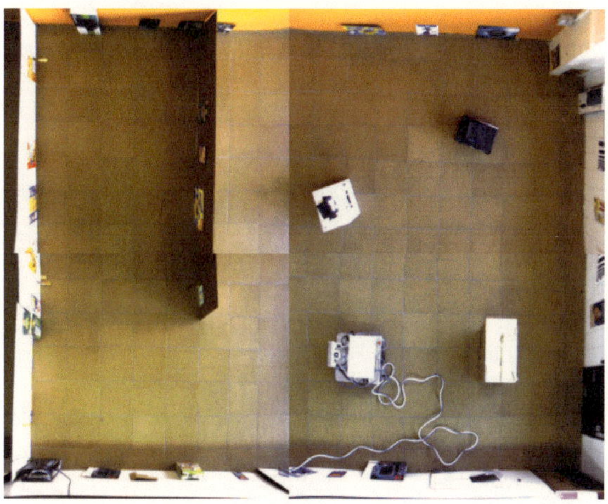

Fig. 13. Overhead view of the real scene of the experiment of figure 12.

Fig. 14. Overhead view of the environment of the experiment of figures 15 and 16.

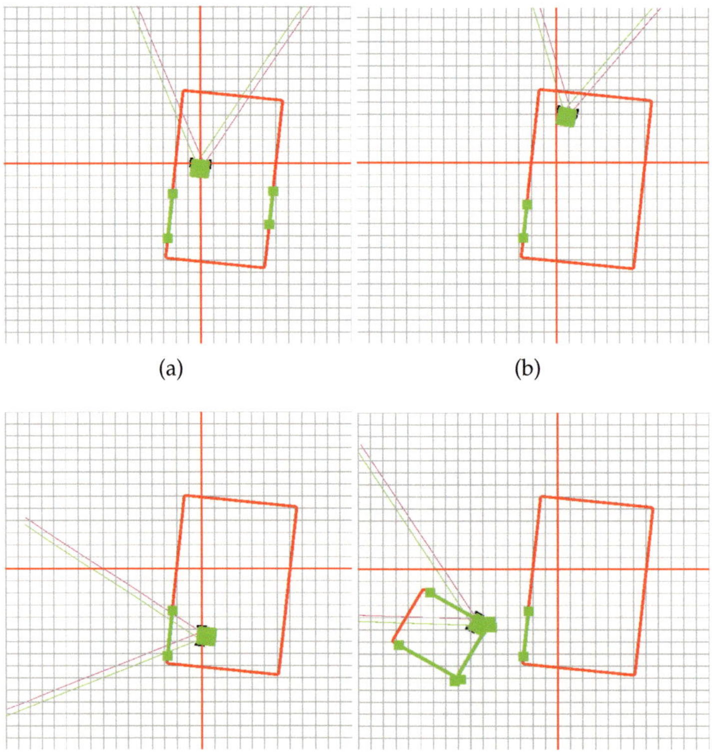

(a) (b)

(c) (d)

Fig. 15. Modeling of the first room during the exploration of the environment of figure 14.

6. Conclusions and future work

In this chapter, we have presented a behavioral architecture for mobile robots endowed with stereo vision that provides them with the ability to actively explore and model their

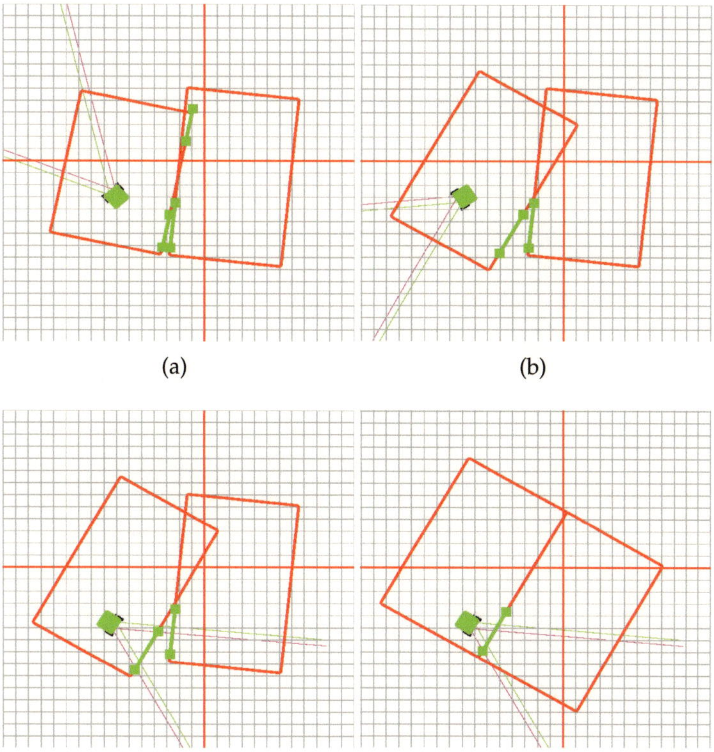

(a) (b)

(c) (d)

Fig. 16. Modeling of the second room during the exploration of the environment of figure 14.

environments. As an initial approach, it is assumed that the environment is formed by rectangular rooms communicated by doors and may contain objects on the floor. The result of the modeling process is a topological graph that represents the set of rooms (nodes) and their connections (edges). Each node in this representation contains the metric description of the corresponding room model. Using this basic metric information robots do not need to maintain in parallel a metric map of the environment. Instead, this metric map can be built whenever it is necessary from the topological representation. Rooms are modeled using a variation of the Hough Transform which detects segments instead of lines. Deviations between room models caused by odometric errors are easily detected and corrected using the geometric restrictions provided by the door connecting them. In addition, we have proposed methods for robot pose estimation as well as for global metric adjustment in loop closings.

The set of perceptual and high-level behaviors needed to solve the active modeling problem are organized according to our attention-based control architecture. In this architecture, attention is conceived as an intermediary between visual perception and action control, solving two fundamental behavioral questions for the robot: *where to look* and *what to do*. Using this scheme, we have defined the different attentional and high-level behaviors that allow the robot to solve the modeling task in an autonomous way. The resulting behavioral system has been tested in real indoor environments of different complexity. These results prove the effectiveness of our proposal in real scenarios.

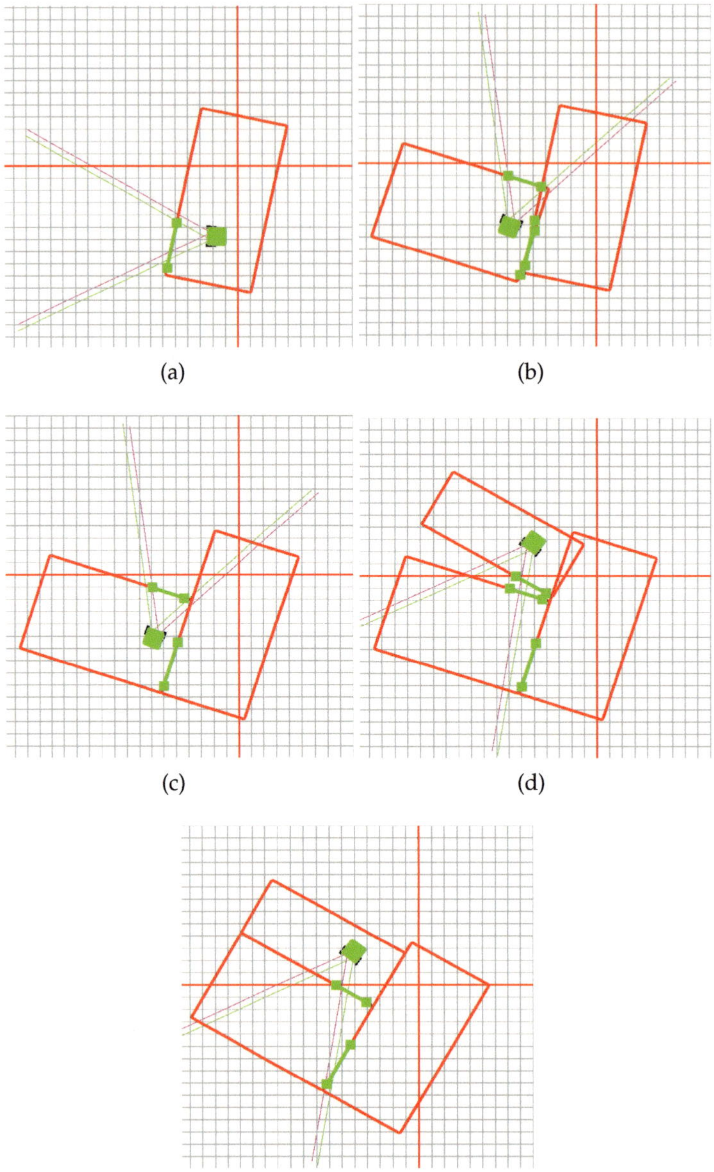

(a) (b) (c) (d) (e)

Fig. 17. Modeling process during an autonomous exploration of the scene of figure 18.

Work in order to relax the *rectangle assumption*, allowing the robot to work with more general models such as *polylines*, is currently in progress. We are also studying the advantages of using formal grammars for topological modeling. In addition, we are also improving and testing the system for much bigger and cluttered environments.

Fig. 18. Overhead view of the real scene of the experiment of figure 17.

7. Acknowledgements

This work has been supported by grant PRI09A037, from the Ministry of Economy, Trade and Innovation of the Extremaduran Government, and by grants TSI-020301-2009-27 and IPT-430000-2010-2, from the Spanish Government and the FEDER funds.

8. References

Allport, A. (1987). Selection for action: Some behavioral and neurophysiological considerations of attention and action, *in* H. Heuer & A. Sanders (eds), *Perspectives on perception and action*, Erlbaum.

Bachiller, P., Bustos, P. & Manso, L. (2008). Attentional selection for action in mobile robots, *in* J. Aramburo & A. R. Trevino (eds), *Advances in robotics, automation and control*, InTech, pp. 111–136.

Duda, R. & Hart, P. (1972). Use of the hough transformation to detect lines and curves in pictures, *Commun. ACM* 15: 11–15.

Enright, J. (1998). Monocularly programmed human saccades during vergence changes?, *Journal of Physiology* 512: 235–250.

Frintrop, S. (2006). *VOCUS: A Visual Attention System for Object Detection and Goal-Directed Search*, Vol. 3899 of *Lecture Notes in Computer Science*, Springer.

Itti, L. & Koch, C. (2000). A saliency-based search mechanism for overt and covert shifts of visual attention, *Vision Research* 40: 1489–1506.

Jung, C. & Schramm, R. (2004). Rectangle detection based on a windowed hough transform, *Proceedins of the XVII Brasilian Symposium on Computer Graphics and Image Processing*, pp. 113–120.

Koch, C. & Ullman, S. (1985). Shifts in selective visual attention: towards the underlying neural circuitry, *Human Neurobiology* 4: 219–227.

Lagunovsky, D. & Ablameyko, S. (1999). Straight-line-based primitive extraction in grey-scale object recognition, *Pattern Recognition Letters* 20(10): 1005–1014.

Lin, C. & Nevatia, R. (1998). Building detection and description from a single intensity image, *Computer Vision and Image Understanding* 72(2): 101–121.

Matas, J., Galambos, C. & Kittler, J. (2000). Robust detection of lines using the progressive probabilistic hough transform, *Computer Vision and Image Understanding* 78(1): 119–137.

Mateos, J., Sánchez-Domínguez, A., Manso, L., Bachiller, P. & Bustos, P. (2010). Robex: an open-hardware robotics platform, *Workshop of Physical Agents*.

Montijano, E. & Sagues, C. (2009). Topological maps based on graphs of planar regions, *IEEE/RSJ International Conference on Intelligent Robots and Systems (IROS)*, pp. 1661–1666.

Navalpakkam, V. & Itti, L. (2006). An integrated model of top-down and bottom-up attention for optimizing detection speed, *CVPR '06: Proceedings of the 2006 IEEE Computer Society Conference on Computer Vision and Pattern Recognition*, IEEE Computer Society, pp. 2049–2056.

Olson, E. (2008). *Robust and Efficient Robotic Mapping*, PhD thesis, Massachusetts Institute of Technology, Cambridge, MA, USA.

Palmer, P., Kittler, J. & Petrou, M. (1994). Using focus of attention with the hough transform for accurate line parameter estimation, *Pattern Recognition* 27(9): 1127–1134.

Robbins, H. & Monro, S. (1951). A stochastic approximation method, *The Annals of Mathematical Statistics* 22(3): 400–407.

Rosenfeld, A. (1969). Picture processing by computer, *ACM Comput. Surv.* 1: 147–176.

Simhon, S. & Dudek, G. (1998). A global topological map formed by local metric maps, *In IEEE/RSJ International Conference on Intelligent Robots and Systems*, pp. 1708–1714.

Tao, W.-B., Tian, J.-W. & Liu, J. (2002). A new approach to extract rectangular building from aerial urban images, *Signal Processing, 2002 6th International Conference on*, Vol. 1, pp. 143 – 146.

Thrun, S. (1998). Learning metric-topological maps for indoor mobile robot navigation, *Artificial Intelligence* 99(1): 21–71.

Tomatis, N., Nourbakhsh, I. & Siegwart, R. (2003). Hybrid simultaneous localization and map building: a natural integration of topological and metric, *Robotics and Autonomous Systems* 44(1): 3–14.

Torralba, A., Oliva, A., Castelhano, M. S. & Henderson, J. M. (2006). Contextual guidance of eye movements and attention in real-world scenes: the role of global features in object search., *Psychol Rev* 113: 766–786.

Van Zwynsvoorde, D., Simeon, T. & Alami, R. (2000). Incremental topological modeling using local voronoï-like graphs, *Proc. of IEEE/RSJ Int. Conf. on Intelligent Robots and System (IROS 2000)*, Vol. 2, pp. 897–902.

Yan, F., Zhuang, Y. & Wang, W. (2006). Large-scale topological environmental model based particle filters for mobile robot indoor localization, *Robotics and Biomimetics, IEEE International Conference on* 0: 858–863.

Zhu, Y., Carragher, B., Mouche, F. & Potter, C. (2003). Automatic particle detection through efficient hough transforms, *IEEE Trans. Med. Imaging* 22(9).

3

Segmentation and Stereoscopic Correspondence in Images Obtained with Omnidirectional Projection for Forest Environments

P. Javier Herrera, Gonzalo Pajares, María Guijarro,
José J. Ruz and Jesús M. de la Cruz
Complutense University of Madrid
Spain

1. Introduction

Stereoscopic vision systems have been used manually for decades to capture three-dimensional information of the environment in different applications. With the growth experienced in recent years by the techniques of computer image processing, stereoscopic vision has been increasingly incorporating automated systems of different nature. The central problem in the automation of a stereoscopic vision system is the determination of the correspondence between pixels of the pair of stereoscopic images that come from the same point in three-dimensional scene.

The research undertaken in this work comprises the design of a global strategy to solve the stereoscopic correspondence problem for a specific kind of hemispherical image from forest environments. The images are obtained through an optical system based on the lens known as fisheye because this optic system can recover 3D information in a large field-of-view around the camera; in our system it is 183°×360°. This is an important advantage because it allows one to image the trees in the 3D scene close to the system from the base to the top, unlike in systems equipped with conventional lenses where close objects are partially mapped (Abraham & Förstner, 2005).

The focus is on obtaining this information from tree trunks using stereoscopic images. The technicians carry out forest inventories which include studies on wood volume and tree density as well as the evolution and growth of the trees with the measurements obtained. Because the trees appear completely imaged, the stereoscopic system allows the calculation of distances from the device to significant points into the trees in the 3D scene, including diameters along the stem, heights and crown dimensions to be measured, as well as determining the position of the trees. These data may be used to obtain precise taper equations, leaf area or volume estimations (Montes et al., 2009). As the distance from the device to each tree can be calculated, the density of trees within a determined area can be also surveyed and growing stock; tree density, basal area (the section of stems at 1.30 m height in a hectare) and other interesting variables may be estimated at forest stand level using statistical inference (Gregoire, 1998).

This work stems from the interest generated by the Spanish Forest Research Centre (CIFOR) part of the National Institute for Agriculture and Food Research and Technology (INIA) to automate the process of extracting information through the measurement mechanism with patent number MU-200501738.

The main contribution of this chapter is the proposal of a strategy that combines the two essential processes involved in artificial stereo vision: segmentation and correspondence of certain structures in the dual images of the stereoscopic pair. The strategy is designed according the type of images used and lighting conditions from forest environments. These refers to Scots pine forests (*Pinus sylvestris* L.) where images were obtained on sunny days and therefore they exhibit highly variable intensity levels due to the illuminated areas. Due to the characteristics of this environment - in terms of light and the nature of trees themselves and textures that surround them - the segmentation and correspondence processes are specifically designed according to this type of forest environment. This sets the trend for future research when analyzing other forest environments. The segmentation process is approached from the point of view of isolating the trunks by excluding the textures that surround them (pine needles, ground and sky). For this reason, we propose the use of the specific techniques of texture identification for the pine needles (Pajares & Cruz, 2007) and of classification for the rest (Pajares et al. 2009; Guijarro et al. 2008, 2009). The correspondence problem can be defined in terms of finding pairs of true matches, as explained below, pixels in two images that are generated by the same physical element in the space. These true matches generally satisfy some constraints (Scharstein & Szeliski, 2002): 1) *epipolar*, given a pixel in an image, the matched pixel in the second image must lie following the called epipolar line; 2) *similarity*, matched pixels must have similar properties or attributes; 3) *ordering*, the relative position between two pixels in an image is preserved in the other image for the corresponding matches; 4) *uniqueness*, each pixel in one image should be matched to a unique pixel in the other image, although a pixel could not be matched because of occlusions. The proposed matching process identifies the homogeneous pixels in separate stereo pair images, by means of the combination of similarity measurements calculated from a set of attributes extracted of each pixel.

The proposed strategy based on segmentation and correspondence processes can be favourably compared from the perspective of the automation of the process and we suggest it can be applied to any type of forest environment, with the appropriate adaptations inherent to the segmentation and correspondence processes in accordance with the nature of the forest environment analyzed.

This chapter is organized as follows. In section 2 we describe the procedures applied for the image segmentation oriented to the identification of textures. Section 3 describes the design of the matching process by applying the epipolar, similarity and uniqueness constraints. Section 4 presents the conclusions and future work.

2. Segmentation

In our approach, the interest is focused on the trunks of the trees because they contain the higher concentration of wood. These are our features of interest in which the matching process is focused. Figure 1 displays a representative hemispherical stereo pair captured with a fisheye lens from the forest. As one can see, there are three main groups of textures without interest, such as grass in the soil, sky in the gaps and leaves of the trees. Hence, the first step consists on the identification of the textures out the interest to be excluded during the matching process. This is carried out through a segmentation process which uses both: a) methods for texture analysis (Gonzalez & Woods, 2008) and b) a classification approach based on the combination of two single classifiers, they are the parametric Bayesian estimator and the Parzen's window (Duda et al., 2001). The first tries to isolate the leaves based on statistical measures and the second classifies the other two kinds of textures. The performance of combined classifiers has been reported as a promising approach against individual classifiers (Kuncheva, 2004; Guijarro et al., 2008, 2009; Pajares et al., 2009; Herrera et al., 2011a).

One might wonder why not to identify the textures belonging to the trunks. The response is simple. This kind of textures displays a high variability of tonalities depending on the orientation of the trunks with respect the sun. Therefore, there is not a unique type of texture (dark or illuminated trunks and even though alternatively in bits), as we can see in Figure 1. Observing the textures we can also see the following: *a*) the areas covered with leaves display high intensity variability in a pixel and the surrounding pixels in its neighbourhood; therefore methods based on detecting this behaviour could be suitable; *b*) on the contrary, the sky displays homogeneous areas, where a pixel is surrounded of pixels with similar intensity values where the dominant spectral visible component is blue; *c*) the grass in the soil also tend to fall on the category of homogeneous textures although with some variability coming from shades, in both shaded and sunny areas the pixels belonging to the grass have the green spectral component as the dominant one; *d*) the textures coming from the trunks are the most difficult as we said above; indeed due to the sun position, the angle of the incident rays from the sun produce strong shades in the part of the trunks in the opposite position of the projection (west part in the images of Figure 1); the trunks receiving the direct projection display a high degree of illumination (east part in the images of Figure 1); there are a lot of trunks where the shades produce different areas.

Based on the above, for identifying the textures coming from leaves, we use texture analysis techniques based on statistical measures that can cope with the high intensity variability. This is explained in section 2.1. Because of the homogeneity of grass and sky textures, we can use methods based on learning approaches as explained in section 2.2. Finally, the textures coming from the trunks are not specifically identified during the segmentation phase and they are processed during the stereovision matching process, described in section 3.

(a) (b)

Fig. 1. A representative hemispherical stereo pair; (a) left image; (b) right image.

2.1 Identification of high contrasted textures

The textures produced by the leaves of the trees under analysis do not display spatial distributions of frequencies nor textured patterns; they are rather high contrasted areas without any spatial orientation. Hence, we have verified that the most appropriate texture descriptors are those capturing the high contrast, i.e. statistical second-order moments. One of the simplest is the variance. It is a measure of intensity contrast defined in our approach as in (Gonzalez & Woods, 2008; Herrera, 2010). The criterion for identifying a high textured area is established by considering that it should have a value for the intensity contrast coefficient R, normalized in the range [0, +1], greater than a threshold T_1, set to 0.8 in this chapter after experimentation. This value is established taking into account that only the areas with large values should be considered, otherwise a high number of pixels could be identified as belonging to these kinds of textures because the images coming from outdoor environments (forests) display a lot of areas with different levels of contrast.

2.2 Identification of homogeneous textures: combining classifiers

Any classification process in general and in particular the identification of textures in natural images has associated two main phases: training and decision. We refer to the first phase as learning phase also, by identifying both concepts in the literature. By the nature of processing in the time sometimes appear as off-line and on-line processes respectively. This is due to the fact that the training phase is usually carried out during system downtime, being at this time when the parameters involved in the process are estimated or learned. However, the decision phase is performed for a fully operational system, using the parameters learned in the training phase.
Figure 2 shows an overview of a training-decision system particularized to the case of natural texture images. Both phases consist of both common and different processes. Indeed, the processes of image capture, segmentation and coding information are common, while learning and decision processes are different. We briefly describe each of them. Then in each method the appropriate differentiation is provided.

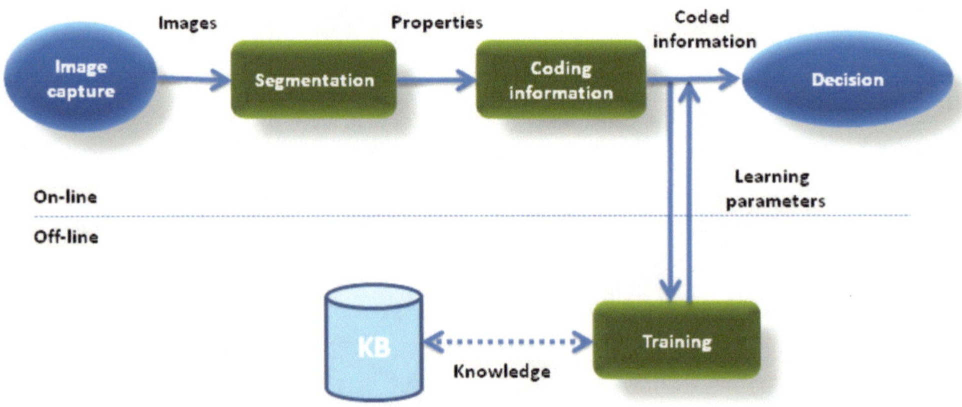

Fig. 2. General scheme of a training-decision process

This scheme is valid for both the individual nature and combined classifiers.

- *Image capture*: it consists in obtaining the images, either obtained from a databank or directly from the scene by the corresponding sensor.

- *Segmentation*: segmentation is the process involving the extraction of structures or features in the images. From the point of view of image treatment, a feature can be a region or an edge that belongs to any object. A feature can also be a pixel belonging to a border, a point of interest or simply a pixel of the image regardless of inside or outside any of the aforementioned structures. In the case of a region can be its area, perimeter, intensity average or any other property describing the region. The pixels are the features used in this work. In our case, the attributes or properties of the pixels will be their spectral components. Consequently, the segmentation process includes both, feature extraction and properties.
- *Coding information*: This phase includes the structuring of the information to be subsequently used by both methods learning and classification. Each feature taken during the previous phase are the samples represented by vectors, whose components are the properties of the feature under analysis. As mentioned previously, the features to consider are the pixels. Given a pixel in the spatial location (*i, j*), if it is labelled as k we have $k \equiv (i,j)$, being x_k the vector whose components are the representative spectral values of that pixel in the *RGB* colour model, i.e. $\mathbf{x}_k = \{x_{k_1}, x_{k_2}, x_{k_3}\} \equiv \{R,G,B\} \in \Re^3$ and therefore, in this case, the vector belongs to the three-dimensional space. The samples are coded for both the training process and the decision process; then we will have training samples and classification samples according to the stage where they are processed.
- *Learning/Training*: with the available samples properly encoded, the training process is carried out according to the method selected. The learning resulting parameters are stored in the Knowledge Base (*KB*), Figure 2, for being used during the decision phase.
- *Identification/Decision*: at this stage we proceed to identify a new feature or sample, which has not yet been classified as belonging to one of the existing classes of interest. To do that the previously learned and stored parameters in KB are retrieved, thereafter through the corresponding decision function, inherent to each method, the class to which it belongs is identified. This process is also called recognition or classification. It is sometimes common that the classified samples can be incorporated back into the system, now as training samples to proceed to a new learning process and therefore to carry out a new updating of the parameters associated to each method, that are stored again in the KB. This is known as incremental learning.

As mentioned before, in our approach there are other two relevant textures that must be identified. They are specifically the sky and the grass. For a pixel belonging to one of such areas the *R* coefficient should be low because of its homogeneity. This is a previous criterion for identifying such areas, where the 'low' concept is mapped assuming that *R* should be less than the previous threshold T_1. Nevertheless, this is not sufficient because there are other different areas which are not sky or grass fulfilling this criterion. Therefore, we apply a classification technique based on the combination of the parametric Bayesian estimator (PB) and Parzen window (PZ) approaches. The choice of these classifiers is based on its proven effectiveness when applied individually in various fields of application, including image classification. According to (Kuncheva, 2004), if they are combined the results improve. Both PB and PZ consist of two phases: training and decision.

2.2.1 Training phase

We start with the observation of a set X of n training patterns, i.e. $X = \{\mathbf{x}_1, \mathbf{x}_2, \ldots, \mathbf{x}_n\} \in \Re^q$. Each sample is to be assigned to a given cluster c_j, where the number of possible clusters is c, i.e. $j = 1, 2,\ldots,c$. In our approach the number of clusters is two, corresponding to grass and sky textures, i.e. $c = 2$. For simplicity, in our experiments, we identify the cluster c_1 with the sky and the cluster c_2 with the grass. The $\boldsymbol{x}_i$ patterns represent pixels in the *RGB* colour space. Their components are the *R,G,B* spectral values. This means, that the dimension of the space $\Re$ is $q = 3$.

a. *Parametric Bayesian Classifier (PB)*

This method has traditionally been identified within the unsupervised classification techniques (Escudero, 1977). Given a generic training sample $\boldsymbol{x} \in \Re^q$, the goal is to estimate the membership probabilities to each class c_j, i.e. $P_1(c_j \mid \boldsymbol{x})$. This technique assumes that the density function of conditional probability for each class is known, resulting unknown the parameters. A widespread practice, adopted in our approach, is to assume that the shape of these functions follows the law of Gaussian or Normal distribution, according to the following expression,

$$p_1(\boldsymbol{x} \mid \boldsymbol{m}_j, C_j) = \frac{1}{(2\pi)^{q/2} \left|C_j\right|^{1/2}} \exp\left\{-\frac{1}{2}(\boldsymbol{x} - \boldsymbol{m}_j)^T C_j^{-1} (\boldsymbol{x} - \boldsymbol{m}_j)\right\} \tag{1}$$

where $\boldsymbol{m}_j$ and C_j are, respectively, the mean and covariance matrix of class c_j, i.e. statistical or unknown parameters to be estimated, T denotes the transposed matrix and q express the dimensionality of the data by $\boldsymbol{x} \in \Re^q$.

The hypotheses assumed by the unsupervised classification techniques are:

1. There are c classes in the problem.
2. The sample $\boldsymbol{x}$ comes from these c classes, although the specific class to which it belongs is unknown.
3. The a priori probability that the sample belongs to class c_j, $P(c_j)$ is in principle unknown.
4. The density function associated with each class has a known form, being unknown the parameters of that function.

With this approach it is feasible to implement the Bayes rule to obtain conditional probability that $\boldsymbol{x}_s$ belongs to class c_j, by the following expression (Huang & Hsu, 2002),

$$P_1(c_j \mid \boldsymbol{x}_s) = \frac{p(\boldsymbol{x}_s \mid \boldsymbol{m}_j, C_j) P(c_j)}{\sum_{j=1}^{c} p(\boldsymbol{x}_s \mid \boldsymbol{m}_j, C_j)} \tag{2}$$

Knowing the shapes of probability density functions, the parametric Bayesian method seeks to estimate the best parameters for these functions.

b. *Parzen window (PZ)*

In this process, as in the case of parametric Bayesian method, the goal remains the estimation of the membership probabilities of sample $\boldsymbol{x}$ to each class c_j, that is $P_2(c_j \mid \boldsymbol{x})$. Therefore, the problem arises from the same point of view, making the same first three hypotheses and replacing the fourth by a new more general: "the shape of the probability density function associated with each class is not known". This means that in this case there are no parameters to be estimated, except the probability density function (Parzen, 1962; Duda et al. 2001). The estimated density function turns out to be that provided by equation

(3), where $D(\cdot) = (\boldsymbol{x} - \boldsymbol{x}_k)^T C_j^{-1} (\boldsymbol{x} - \boldsymbol{x}_k) / 2h_j^2$, q represents the dimension of the samples in the space considered, T indicates the vector transpose operation.

$$p_2(x \mid c_j) = \frac{1}{n_j} \sum_{k=1}^{n_j} \left\{ \frac{\exp\{-D(x, x_k, h_j)\}}{(2\pi)^{q/2} h_j^{n_j} |C_j|^{1/2}} \right\} \tag{3}$$

According to equation (3), this classifier estimates the density function probability given the training samples associated with each class, requiring that the samples are distributed, i.e. the partition must be available. Also the covariance matrices associated with each of the classes are used. The full partition and covariance matrices are the parameters that this classifier stored in the KB during the training phase. In fact, the covariance matrices are the same as those obtained by PB.

During the decision phase, PZ extracts from KB both the covariance matrices C_j and the available training samples are distributed in their respective classes. With them the probability density function given in equation (3) is generated. Thus, from a new sample $\boldsymbol{x}_s$ conditional probabilities are obtained according to this equation, $P_2(\boldsymbol{x}_s \mid c_j)$. The probability that the sample $\boldsymbol{x}_s$ belongs to the class w_j can be obtained by again applying Bayes rule,

$$P_2(c_j \mid x_s) = \frac{p_2(x_s \mid c_j) P(c_j)}{\sum_{j=1}^{c} p_2(x_s \mid c_j)} \tag{4}$$

2.2.2 Decision phase

After the training phase, a new unclassified sample $\boldsymbol{x}_s \in \Re^q$ must be classified as belonging to a cluster c_j. Here, each sample, like each training sample, represents a pixel at the image with the R,G,B components. PB computes the probabilities that $\boldsymbol{x}_s$ belong to each cluster from equation (2) and PZ computes the probabilities that $\boldsymbol{x}_s$ belong to each cluster from equation (4). Both probabilities are the outputs of the individual classifiers ranging in [0,1]. They are combined by using the *mean rule* (Kuncheva, 2004). (Tax et al., 2000) compare performances of combined classifiers by averaging and multiplying. As reported there, combining classifiers which are trained in independent feature spaces result in improved performance for the product rule, while in completely dependent feature spaces the performance is the same for the product and the average. In our RGB feature space high correlation among the R, G and B spectral components exists (Littmann & Ritter, 1997; Cheng et al., 2001). High correlation means that if the intensity changes, all the three components will change accordingly. Therefore we chose the mean for the combination, which is computed as: $m_{sj} = (P_1(c_j \mid \boldsymbol{x}_s) + P_2(c_j \mid \boldsymbol{x}_s))/2$. The pixel represented by $\boldsymbol{x}_s$ is classified according to the following decision rule: $\boldsymbol{x}_s \in c_j$ if $m_{sj} > m_{sh}$ and $m_{sj} > T_2$ otherwise the pixel remains unclassified. We have added, to the above rule, the second term with the logical *and* operator involving the threshold T_2 because we are only identifying pixels belonging to the sky or grass clusters. This means that the pixels belonging to textures different from the previous ones remain unclassified, and they become candidates for the stereo matching process. The threshold T_2 has been set to 0.8 after experimentation. This is a relative high value, which identifies only pixels with a high membership degree in either c_1 or c_2. We have preferred to exclude only pixels which belong clearly to one of the above two textures.

Figure 3(b) displays the result of applying the segmentation process to the left image in Figure 3(a). The white areas are identified either as textures belonging to sky and grass or leaves of the trees. On the contrary, the black zones, inside the circle defining the image, are the pixels to be matched. As one can see the majority of the trunks are black, they really represent the pixels of interest to be matched through the corresponding correspondence process. There are white trunks representing trees very far from the sensor. They are not considered because are out of our interest from the point of view of forest inventories.

Fig. 3. (a) Original left image; (b) segmented left image where white areas are textures without interest (sky, grass and leaves) and the black ones the pixels to be matched.

It is difficult to validate the results obtained by the segmentation process, but we have verified that without this process, the error for stereovision matching strategies is increased by a quantity that represents on average about 9-10 percentage points. In addition to this quantitative improvement it is easy to deduce the existence of a qualitative improvement by the fact that some pixels belonging to textures not excluded by the absence of segmentation, they are incorrectly matched with pixels belonging to the trunks, this do not occur when these textures are excluded because they were not offered this possibility. This means that the segmentation is a fundamental process in our stereovision system and justifies its application.

3. Stereovision matching

Once the image segmentation process is finished, we have identified pixels belonging to three types of textures which are to be discarded during the next stereovision matching process, because they are without interest. Hence, we only apply the stereovision matching process to the pixels that do not belong to any of the previous textures. As we explained before, due to the different locations of the tree's crowns there exists an important lighting variability between both images of the stereoscopic pair; this makes the matching process a difficult task.

As mentioned in section 1, in stereovision there are several constraints that can be applied. In our approach we apply three of them: epipolar, similarity and uniqueness. Given a pixel in the left image, we apply the epipolar constraint for determining a list of candidates, which are potential matches in the right image. Each candidate becomes an alternative for the first pixel. Through the combination of similarity measurements computed from a set of attributes extracted of each pixel (similarity constraint), we obtain the final decision about the best match among candidates by applying the uniqueness constraint. Epipolar constraint is explained in section 3.1 and similarity and uniqueness constraints in section 3.2.

3.1 Epipolar constraint: system geometry

Figure 4 displays the stereovision system geometry (Abraham & Förstner, 2005). The 3D object point P with world coordinates with respect to the systems (X_1, Y_1, Z_1) and (X_2, Y_2, Z_2) is imaged as (x_{i1}, y_{i1}) and (x_{i2}, y_{i2}) in image-1 and image-2 respectively in coordinates of the image system; α_1 and α_2 are the angles of incidence of the rays from P; y_{12} is the baseline measuring the distance between the optical axes along the y-axes with respect to the two positions of the camera; r is the distance between the image point and the optical axis; R is the image radius, identical in both images.

According to (Schwalbe, 2005), the following geometrical relations can be established,

$$r = \sqrt{x_{i1}^2 + y_{i1}^2}\ ;\ \alpha_1 = (r90^{\circ})/R\ ;\ \beta = tg^{-1}(y_{i1}/x_{i1}) \tag{5}$$

Now the problem is that the 3D world coordinates (X_1, Y_1, Z_1) are unknown. They can be estimated by varying the distance d as follows,

$$X_1 = d\cos\beta\ ;\ Y_1 = d\sin\beta\ ;\ Z_1 = \sqrt{X_1^2 + Y_1^2}\Big/\tan\alpha_1 \tag{6}$$

From (6) we transform the world coordinates in the system $O_1X_1Y_1Z_1$ to the world coordinates in the system $O_2X_2Y_2Z_2$ taking into account the baseline as follows,

$$X_2 = X_1\ ;\ Y_2 = Y_1 + y_{12}\ ;\ Z_2 = Z_1 \tag{7}$$

Assuming that the lenses have no radial distortion, we can find the imaged coordinates of the 3D point in image-2 as (Schwalbe, 2005),

$$x_{i2} = \frac{2R\arctan\left(\sqrt{X_2^2 + Y_2^2}\Big/Z_2\right)}{\pi\sqrt{(Y_2/X_2)^2 + 1}}\ ;\ y_{i2} = \frac{2R\arctan\left(\sqrt{X_2^2 + Y_2^2}\Big/Z_2\right)}{\pi\sqrt{(X_2/Y_2)^2 + 1}} \tag{8}$$

Using only a camera or a camera position, we capture a unique image and the 3D points belonging to the line $\overline{O_1P}$ are all imaged in the unique point (x_{i1}, y_{i1}). So, the 3D coordinates cannot be obtained from a single image. When we try to match the imaged point (x_{i1}, y_{i1}) into the image-2 we follow the epipolar line, i.e. the projection of $\overline{O_1P}$ over the image-2. This is equivalent to varying the parameter *d* in the 3-D space. So, given the imaged point (x_{i1}, y_{i1}) in image-1 (left) and following the epipolar line, we obtain a list of *m* potential corresponding candidates represented by (x_{i2}, y_{i2}) in image-2 (right).

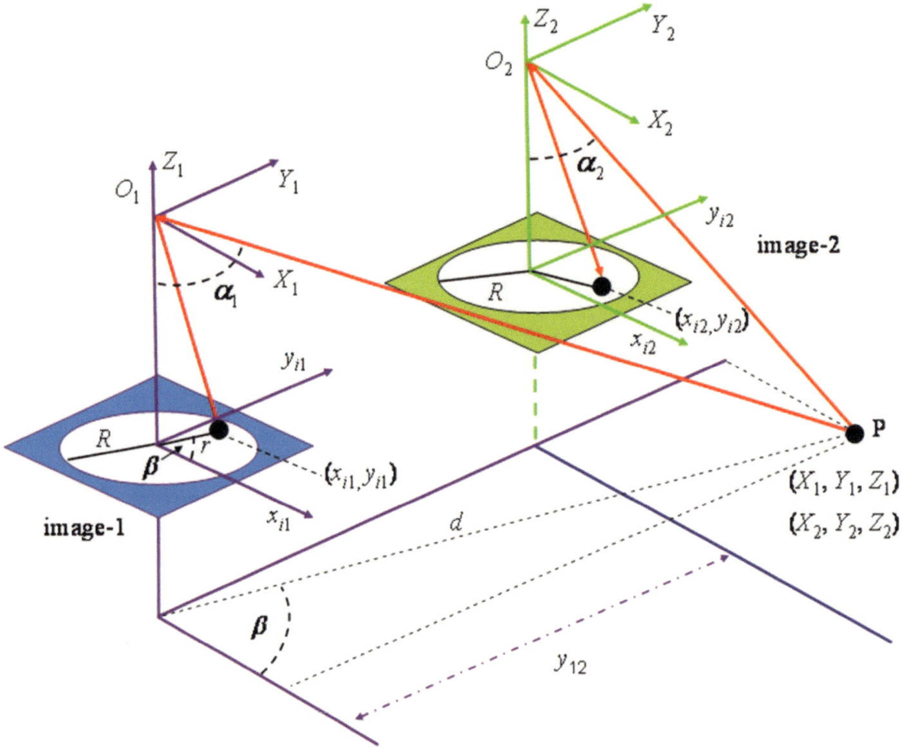

Fig. 4. Geometric projections and relations for the fisheye based stereo vision system.

3.2 Similarity and uniqueness constraints

Each pixel *l* in the left image is characterized by its attributes; one of such attributes is denoted as A_l. In the same way, each candidate *i* in the list of *m* candidates is described by identical attributes, A_i. So, we can compute differences between attributes of the same type *A*, obtaining a similarity measure for each attribute as,

$$s_{iA} = 1/\left(1 + |A_l - A_i|\right); \quad i = 1,\dots,m \tag{9}$$

$s_{iA} \in [0,1]$, $s_{iA} = 0$ if the difference between attributes is large enough (minimum similarity), otherwise if they are equal ($s_{iA} = 1$, maximum similarity).

In this chapter, we use the following five attributes for describing each pixel (feature): *a*) Gabor filter; *b*) variance as a measure of the texture; *c*) RGB color; *d*) CIE lab color and *e*) gradient magnitude. The first two are area-based computed on a 3×3 neighborhood around each pixel (Pajares & Cruz, 2007). The latter three are considered as feature-based (Lew et al., 1994). Gabor filter is basically a bi-dimensional Gaussian function centered at origin (0,0) with variance S modulated by a complex sinusoid with polar frequency (F,W) and phase P. The RGB color involves the three Red-Green-Blue spectral components and the absolute value in equation (9) is extended as: $|A_l - A_i| = \sum_H |H_l - H_i|$, H = R,G,B. In the same way, the CIE lab color involves the three *l-a-b* components and the absolute value in equation (9) is extended as: $|A_l - A_i| = \sum_H |H_l - H_i|$, $H = l,a,b$. Gradient magnitude is computed by applying the first derivative (Pajares & Cruz, 2007), over the intensity image after its transformation from the RGB plane to the HSI (hue, saturation, intensity) one.

Other attributes have been unsuccessfully used in previous works in the same forest environment, e.g. correlation, gradient direction and Laplacian (Herrera, 2010; Herrera et al., 2011a, 2011b). While gradient magnitude, RGB color and texture obtained the best individual results, respectively. For this reason they are used in this work.

Given a pixel in the left image and the set of m candidates in the right one, we compute the following similarity measures for each attribute A: s_{ia} (Gabor filter), s_{ib} (texture), s_{ic} (RGB color), s_{id} (CIE lab color) and s_{ie} (gradient magnitude). The identifiers in the sub-indices identify the attributes according to the above assignments.

Now we must match each pixel l in the left image with the best of the potential candidates (uniqueness constraint). This is based on a majority voting criterion (MVC). So, given l and its i candidates, we have available s_{ia}, s_{ib}, s_{ic}, s_{id} and s_{ie}, so that we can make individual decisions about the best candidate i based on maximum similarity measurements among the set of candidates. We determine the best match by choosing the candidates with the maximum similarity for each individual attribute and select the one which has been chosen according to the majority of attributes. Each one of the five attributes, used separately, allows determining a disparity map for comparison purposes.

The sexagesimal system is used in measuring angles. The practical unit of angular measure is the degree, of which there are 360 in a circle. The disparity value at each pixel location is the absolute difference value in sexagesimal degrees between the angle for the pixel in the left image and the angle of its matched pixel in the right one. Each pixel is given in polar coordinates with respect the centre of the image.

Given a stereo pair of the twenty used for testing, for each pixel we obtain its disparity as follows. Considering the five attributes separately, used as criteria in the MVC, and applying a maximum similarity criterion according to equation (9) among the m candidates, we obtain a disparity map for each attribute. So, for comparative purposes we show for the area in Figure 5(b), the disparity maps obtained by Gabor Filter, texture, RGB and CIE lab colors, and gradient magnitude in Figures 5(c) to 5(g), respectively. By applying the MVC approach based on maximum similarity, we obtain the disparity map displayed in Figure 5(h). The color bar in Figure 5(i) shows the disparity level values according to the color for each disparity map.

An important observation comes from the main trunk in the Figure 5(b); indeed, in the corresponding disparity maps obtained by Gabor filter and texture, the disparity values range from 1.5 to 5.5, but in RGB and CIE lab colors, and gradient magnitude they range from 3.5 to 5.5. In the disparity map obtained by MVC strategy, the low level values have been removed, such that the disparities range from 4.5 to 5.5. Although there are still several disparity levels, this is correct because the trunk is very thick and it is placed near the sensor. This assertion is verified by the expert human criterion.

The best individual results, according to the five attributes, are obtained through the similarities provided by the gradient magnitude (s_{ie}). This implies that it is the most relevant attribute. Nevertheless, the main relevant results are obtained by the proposed MVC approach in terms of less percentage of error. This together with the qualitative improvement provided by this approach, as explained above, allows us to conclude that this is a suitable method for computing the disparity map in this kind of images.

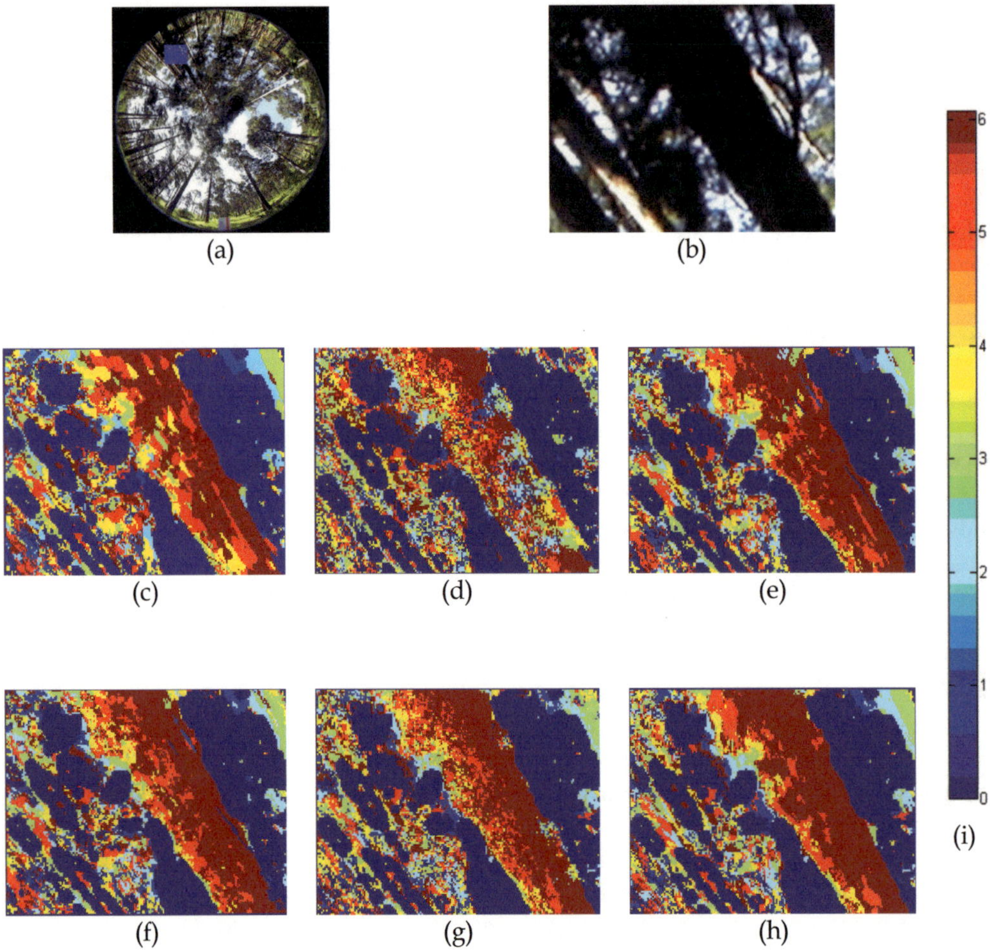

Fig. 5. (a) Hemispherical left image; (b) left expanded area corresponding to the blue signed area in (a); disparity maps obtained by (c) Gabor filter, (d) texture, (e) RGB color, (f) CIE lab color, (g) gradient magnitude, (h) MVC; (i) color bar shows the disparity level values according to the color for each disparity map.

Other combined decision making approaches have been successfully used in previous works in the same forest environment, where the final decision about the correct match, among the candidates in the list, is made according to techniques used for combining classifiers conveniently adapted in our approach to be applied for the stereovision matching (Herrera et al., 2009a, 2009b, 2009c, 2011b; Herrera, 2010; Pajares et al., 2011). In (Herrera et al., 2011a) the similarity and uniqueness constraints are mapped through a decision making strategy based on a weighted fuzzy similarity approach.

4. Conclusions

This chapter presents segmentation and matching strategies for obtaining a disparity map from hemispherical stereo images captured with fisheye lenses. This is carried out through a segmentation process which uses the combination of the parametric Bayesian estimator and the Parzen's window classifiers and the variance as method for texture analysis. The goal of the image segmentation process is to classify and exclude the pixels belonging to one of the three kinds of textures without interest in the images: sky, grass in the soil and leaves. The combined classification strategy classifies sky and grass textures and the variance tries to isolate the leaves based on statistical measures. The exclusion of these textures is useful because the errors that they could introduce during the correspondence can be considerably reduced. While others individual classifiers might have been chosen as a different combined strategy, as the Fuzzy Clustering, the Generalized Lloyd algorithm and the Self-Organizing Maps (Pajares & Cruz, 2007), the combination of both in relation to the improvement of the results according to the set of images used shows its promising possibilities. All this does not preclude the future use of new classifiers and the combination of other strategies for the type of images analyzed.

Once the image segmentation process is finished, an initial disparity map is obtained by applying three stereovision matching constraints (epipolar, similarity and uniqueness). For each pixel in the left image, a list of possible candidates in the right one is obtained for determining its correspondence. This is carried out through a majority voting criterion, which is a decision strategy based on combining similarity measurements from five attributes extracted of each pixel. The proposed combined strategy outperforms the methods that use similarities separately. Based on this, some optimization approaches could be used, such as simulated annealing or Hopfield neural networks, where the smoothness constraint and the Gestalt's principles could be applied under an energy minimization based process.

The method proposed can be applied for similar forest environments where pixels are the key features to be matched. Applications using this sensor are based on identical geometry and image projection, although the matching strategy could be completely different. This occurs in (Herrera et al., 2009d), based on region segmentation where the images are very different and captured under different illumination conditions in Rebollo oak forests.

5. Acknowledgments

The authors wish to acknowledge to the Council of Education of the Autonomous Community of Madrid and the Social European Fund for the research contract with the first author. Also to Drs. Fernando Montes and Isabel Cañellas from the Forest Research Centre (CIFOR-INIA) for their support and the imaged material supplied. This chapter was prepared with economical support of the European Community, the European Union and CONACYT under grant FONCICYT 93829. The content of this document is an exclusive responsibility of the Complutense University, and cannot be considered as the position of the European Community. This chapter has also been partially funded under project DPI2009-14552-C02-01 from the Ministerio de Educación y Ciencia of Spain within the Plan Nacional of I+D+i.

6. References

Abraham, S. & Förstner, W. (2005). Fish-eye-stereo calibration and epipolar rectification. *Photogrammetry and Remote Sensing*, Vol.59, pp. 278-288, ISSN 0924-2716

Cheng, H.D., Jiang, X.H., Sun, Y. & Wang, J. (2001). Color image segmentation: advances and prospects. *Pattern Recognition*, Vol.34, No.12, pp. 2259–2281, ISSN 0031-3203

Duda, R.O., Hart, P.E. & Stork, D.S. (2001). *Pattern Classification* (2nd edition), Wiley & Sons, ISBN 978-04-710-5669-0, New York, USA

Escudero, L.F. (1977). *Reconocimiento de patrones*, Paraninfo, ISBN 978-84-283-0898-4, Madrid, Spain

Gonzalez, R.C. & Woods, R.E. (2008). *Digital Image Processing* (3rd edition), Prentice Hall, ISBN 978-01-316-8728-8, New Jersey, USA

Gregoire, T.G. (1998). Design-based and model-based inference in survey sampling: appreciating the difference. *Canadian Journal of Forest Research*, Vol.28, pp. 1429–1447, ISSN 0045-5067

Guijarro, M., Pajares, G. & Herrera, P.J. (2009). Image-Based Airborne Sensors: A Combined Approach for Spectral Signatures Classification through Deterministic Simulated Annealing. *Sensors*, Vol.9, No.9, pp. 7132-7149, ISSN 1424-8220

Guijarro, M., Pajares, G. & Herrera, P.J. (2008). On Combining Classifiers by Relaxation for Natural Textures in Images, In: *Lecture Notes in Artificial Intelligecnce 5271*, E. Corchado, A. Abraham & W. Pedrycz (Eds.), 345-352, Springer-Verlag, ISBN 978-3-540-87656-4, Berlin, Germany

Herrera, P.J., Pajares, G., Guijarro, M., Ruz, J.J. & Cruz, J.M. (2011a). A Stereovision Matching Strategy for Images Captured with Fish-Eye Lenses in Forest Environments. *Sensors*, Vol.11, pp. 1756-1783, ISSN 1424-8220

Herrera, P.J., Pajares, G., Guijarro, M., Ruz, J.J. & Cruz, J.M. (2011b). Combining Support Vector Machines and simulated annealing for stereovision matching with fish eye lenses in forest environments. *Expert Systems with Applications*, Vol.38, pp. 8622–8631, ISSN 0957-4174

Herrera, P.J. (2010). *Correspondencia estereoscópica en imágenes obtenidas con proyección omnidireccional para entornos forestales*. PhD Dissertation (in Spanish), Faculty of Computer Science, Complutense University of Madrid, 2010.

Herrera, P.J., Pajares, G., Guijarro, M., Ruz, J.J. & Cruz, J.M. (2009a). Choquet Fuzzy Integral applied to stereovision matching for fish-eye lenses in forest analysis, In: *Advances in Soft Computing 61*, W. Yu & E.N. Sanchez (Eds.), 179–187, Springer-Verlag, ISBN 978-3-642-03156-4, Berlin, Germany

Herrera, P.J., Pajares, G., Guijarro, M., Ruz, J.J. & Cruz, J.M. (2009b). Combination of attributes in stereovision matching for fish-eye lenses in forest analysis, In: *Lecture Notes in Computer Science 5807*, J. Blanc-Talon et al. (Eds.), 277-287, Springer-Verlag, ISBN 978-3-642-04697-1, Berlin, Germany

Herrera, P.J., Pajares, G., Guijarro, M., Ruz, J.J. & Cruz, J.M. (2009c). Fuzzy Multi-Criteria Decision Making in Stereovision Matching for Fish-Eye Lenses in Forest Analysis, In: *Lecture Notes in Computer Science 5788*, H. Yin & E. Corchado (Eds.), 325-332, Springer-Verlag, ISBN 978-3-642-04394-9, Berlin, Germany

Herrera, P.J., Pajares, G., Guijarro, M., Ruz, J.J., Cruz, J.M. & Montes, F. (2009d). A Featured-Based Strategy for Stereovision Matching in Sensors with Fish-Eye Lenses for Forest Environments. *Sensors*, Vol.9, pp. 9468-9492, ISSN 1424-8220

Huang, H.J. & Hsu, C.N. (2002). Bayesian classification for data from the same unknown class. *IEEE Transactions on Systems, Man, and Cybernetics*, Part B, Vol.32, No.2, pp. 137-145, ISSN 1083-4419.

Kuncheva, L. (2004). *Combining Pattern Classifiers: Methods and Algorithms*, Wiley, ISBN 978-0-471-21078-8, New Jersey, USA

Lew, M.S., Huang, T.S. & Wong, K. (1994). Learning and feature selection in stereo matching. *IEEE Transactions on Pattern Analysis and Machine Intelligence*, Vol.16, pp. 869–881, ISSN 0162-8828.

Littmann, E. & Ritter, H. (1997). Adaptive color segmentation -A comparison of neural and statistical methods. *IEEE Transactions on Neural Networks*, Vol.8, No.1, pp. 175-185, ISSN 1045-9227.

Montes, F., Ledo, A., Rubio, A., Pita, P. & Cañellas, I. (2009). Use of estereoscopic hemispherical images for forest inventories, *Proceedings of the International Scientific Conference Forest, Wildlife and Wood Sciences for Society development*, Faculty of Forestry and Wood Sciences, Czech University of Life Sciences, Prague, Czech Republic.

Pajares, G, Herrera, P.J. & Cruz, J.M. (2011). Combining Stereovision Matching Constraints for Solving the Correspondence Problem, In: *Advances in Theory and Applications of Stereo Vision*, Asim Bhatti (Ed.), ISBN: 978-953-307-516-7, InTech, Available from:
http://www.intechopen.com/articles/show/title/combining-stereovision-matching-constraints-for-solving-the-correspondence-problem

Pajares, G., Guijarro, M., Herrera, P.J. & Ribeiro, A. (2009). Combining Classifiers through Fuzzy Cognitive Maps in natural images. *IET Computer Vision*, Vol.3, No.3, pp. 112-123, ISSN 1751-9632.

Pajares, G. & Cruz, J.M. (2007). *Visión por Computador: Imágenes digitales y aplicaciones* (2nd edition), RA-MA, ISBN 978-84-7897-831-1, Madrid, Spain

Parzen, E. (1962). On estimation of a probability density function and mode. *The Annals of Mathematical Statistics*, Vol.33, No.3, pp. 1065-1076, ISSN 0003-4851.

Scharstein, D. & Szeliski, R. (2002). A Taxonomy and evaluation of dense two-frame stereo correspondence algorithms. *International Journal of Computer Vision*, Vol.47, No.1-3, pp. 7–42, ISSN 0920-5691

Schwalbe, E. (2005). Geometric modelling and calibration of fisheye lens camera systems, *Proceedings of the ISPRS working group V/5 'Panoramic Photogrammetry Workshop', Int. Archives of Photogrammetry, Remote Sensing and Spatial Information Sciences*, Vol. 36, Part 5/W8, ISSN 1682-1750, Berlin, Germany, February 2005

Tax, D.M.J., Breukelen, van M., Duin, R.P.W. & Kittler, J. (2000). Combining multiple classifiers by averaging or by multiplying?. *Pattern Recognition*, Vol.33, pp. 1475-1485, ISSN 0031-3203

4

Towards a Biologically Plausible Stereo Approach

José R.A. Torreão and Silvia M.C. Victer
Universidade Federal Fluminense
Brazil

1. Introduction

A computational model for stereoscopic disparity estimation has been recently introduced which reformulates, in neurophysiologically plausible terms, the traditional image matching approach (Torreão, 2007). The left and right stereo images are assumed viewed through the receptive fields of cortical simple cells, modeled as Gabor functions (Marcelja, 1980). The Green's functions of a matching equation (whose uniform solutions are also Gabor functions) are used to filter the receptive-field modulated inputs, introducing different relative shifts between them. A measure of the local degree of matching of such shifted inputs can then be used for the estimation of stereoscopic disparities, in a way which is reminiscent of the energy model for the responses of cortical complex cells (Adelson & Bergen, 1985; Ohzawa et al., 1997).

Although based on well-established neurophysiological concepts, the Green's function approach is still far from being biologically plausible. For instance, it assumes as cortical inputs the original irradiance images, disregarding the transformations performed by the earlier stages of the visual pathway – namely, the retina and the lateral geniculate nucleus. As a further step towards a fully biological stereo, we here introduce an improved version of the algorithm in (Torreão, 2007), incorporating a new concept of signal coding by input-dependent receptive fields (Torreão et al., 2009).

The classical receptive field description, which assumes a fixed, stimulus-independent spatial organization, has recently been challenged by neurophysiological indications that the receptive-field structure does change with neuronal input (Allman et al., 1985; Bair, 2005; David et al., 2004). In (Torreão et al., 2009), a signal coding scheme has been introduced, where the parameters of the coding functions are obtained from the Fourier transform of the coded signal, and, in (Torreão & Victer, 2010), such scheme has been taken up as a model for stimulus-dependent center-surround (CS) receptive fields, such as those found in the retina and in the lateral geniculate nucleus. Assuming that the role of the CS structures is that of decorrelating natural images, as suggested in (Attick & Redlich, 1992) and (Dan et al., 1996), center-surround receptive fields which code whitened versions of the input signals have been obtained. We show that, by incorporating a similar center-surround coding module into the Green's function stereo algorithm, we are able to obtain better quality disparity estimates, through an approach which is closer to the neurophysiological situation.

This chapter is organized as follows. In Section 2, we review the Green's function disparity estimation approach. Next, we present the stimulus-dependent model for cortical and center-surround receptive fields (Section 3), and in Section 4 we couple the latter with the Green's function stereo. The chapter ends with our concluding remarks.

2. Green's function stereoscopy

The estimation of binocular disparities is a key issue for stereo processing, both in natural and in artificial vision. Binocular disparities arise from positional differences of scene features projected in the two retinae, or in the two cameras of a binocular system. The computational approach for disparity estimation which seems more firmly grounded on neurophysiological findings is the one based on the energy model for cortical cells (Ohzawa et al., 1997). According to this model, a quadrature pair of *simple* cells responsive to the stimulation of either eye (*binocular* cells) filter the stereo images through their receptive fields, modeled by Gabor functions (Marcelja, 1980). The squared magnitude of the output of the quadrature pair is then assumed to constitute the stereo response of the *complex* cortical cell feeding on the pair. By considering a population of such model complex cells, it has been possible to obtain disparity estimates both from synthetic and from real-world stereograms (Chen & Qian, 2004; Qian, 1994).

In (Torreão, 2007), an alternative approach for disparity estimation, preserving most of the neurophysiologically plausible features of the energy model, has been introduced, starting from an image matching equation. In stereoscopy, assuming that the epipolar geometry is known, the matching equation takes a one-dimensional form, such as

$$I_l(x+U,y) = I_r(x,y) \tag{1}$$

where $U \equiv U(x,y)$ denotes the disparity field, and where I_l and I_r stand for the left and the right input images. Typically, an equation such as (1) is employed for the estimation of $U(x,y)$, given the stereo pair, but in (Torreão, 2007) it was taken as a constraint over the matching images, such that, given I_r, its perfect match is to be found, for simple forms of the disparity field.

2.1 Uniform disparity field

For instance, assuming uniform disparity, $U(x) = u$, where u is a constant, we can take a second-order Taylor series expansion of Eq. (1), to obtain

$$\frac{u^2}{2} I_l''(x) + u I_l'(x) + I_l(x) = I_r(x) \tag{2}$$

where the primes denote differentiation with respect to x (for simplicity, we henceforth omit the dependences on y). Eq. (2) can then be solved via the Green's function approach (Torreão et al., 2007), to yield

$$I_l(x) \approx I_r(x-u) = \int_{-\infty}^{\infty} G_u(x,x_0) I_r(x_0) dx_0 \tag{3}$$

where

$$G_u(x,x_0) \equiv G_u(x-x_0) = \begin{cases} \frac{2}{u} \sin\left(\frac{x-x_0}{u}\right) e^{-\left(\frac{x-x_0}{u}\right)}, & \text{if } x > x_0 \\ 0, & \text{if } x < x_0 \end{cases} \tag{4}$$

is the Green's function of Eq. (2), which amounts to the solution to that equation when its right-hand side is the impulse function, $\delta(x - x_0)$ (we are here assuming an unbounded image domain: $x \in [-\infty, \infty]$).
From Eq. (3) we then find that, to second order in u, convolving the right image, $I_r(x)$, with the Green's function $G_u(x)$ effects a shift of that image, to the right, by the fixed amount u. Similarly, the convolution with $G_u(-x)$ (keeping u as a positive parameter) would effect a similar shift to the left. More generally, we can consider a complex Green's kernel, by introducing the quadrature pair to $G_u(x - x_0)$, given as

$$H_u(x - x_0) = \begin{cases} \frac{2}{u} \cos\left(\frac{x-x_0}{u}\right) e^{-\left(\frac{x-x_0}{u}\right)}, & \text{if } x > x_0 \\ 0, & \text{if } x < x_0 \end{cases} \tag{5}$$

which yields a homogeneous solution to Eq. (2) – that is to say, a solution to that equation when its right-hand side is identically zero.
Thus, being

$$K_u(x - x_0) = G_u(x - x_0) + iH_u(x - x_0) \tag{6}$$

the complex Green's kernel, we would obtain, for the rightwards shifted version of $I_r(x)$,

$$I_r(x - u) = \int_{-\infty}^{\infty} K_u(x - x_0) I_r(x_0) dx_0 \tag{7}$$

up to second order in u.

2.2 Linear disparity field

The disparity estimation approach of (Torreão, 2007) is based on a similar Green's kernel as that of Eq. (6), but for a differential equation which approximates a linear matching constraint, that is to say, one for which the disparity field takes the form $U(x) = u + vx$, for u and v constants. More specifically, a rightwards shift is there performed by the complex kernel

$$K(x, x_0) = \begin{cases} 2ke^{[ik(x-x_0)]} e^{-\left[\frac{(x+a)^2-(x_0+a)^2}{2\sigma^2}\right]}, & \text{if } x > x_0 \\ 0, & \text{if } x < x_0 \end{cases} \tag{8}$$

where σ and a are positive constants, and $k = a/\sigma^2$. The kernel $K(x, x_0)$ is the complex Green's function to the equation

$$\frac{1}{2}\left(\frac{\sigma^2}{a}\right)^2 I_l''(x) + \left(\frac{\sigma^2}{a} + \frac{\sigma^2}{a^2}x\right) I_l'(x) + \left(1 + \frac{x^2 + 2ax + \sigma^2}{2a^2}\right) I_l(x) = I_r(x) \tag{9}$$

whose homogeneous solution is the Gabor function $e^{ikx} e^{-\frac{(x+a)^2}{2\sigma^2}}$.
When $|x|$ and σ are both much smaller than a, Eq. (9) can be approximated as

$$\frac{1}{2}\left(\frac{\sigma^2}{a}\right)^2 I_l''(x) + \left(\frac{\sigma^2}{a} + \frac{\sigma^2}{a^2}x\right) I_l'(x) + I_l(x) = I_r(x) \tag{10}$$

which, up to first order in σ^2/a, corresponds to an image matching equation for the linear displacement field

$$U(x) = \frac{\sigma^2}{a} + \frac{\sigma^2}{a^2}x \quad (11)$$

Similarly as in the uniform case, a leftwards image shift would be effected, in this linear disparity model, by the kernel $K^{(-)}(x, x_0) = K(-x, -x_0)$.

2.3 Green's function disparity estimation

Disparity estimation, in the Green's function approach, proceeds thus: the input images, I_l and I_r, are each multiplied by a Gabor function, yielding complex signals. These are then filtered, respectively, by the $K(x, x_0)$ and the $K^{(-)}(x, x_0)$ kernels, which effect spatial shifts and phase changes in the Gabor-modulated inputs (see below). The optimal spatial shift at each image location can thus be obtained by evaluating the match of the filtered images when different values of the kernel parameters are employed. This yields an estimate of the disparity map encoded by the stereo pair.

The relation of the Green's function approach to the neurophysiological models of stereoscopy stems from the following property of the Green's kernels: when filtering a Gabor-function modulated signal, they yield similarly modulated outputs, but for spatially shifted versions of the signal. For instance, let us consider the result of filtering the complex signal

$$I_1(x) = e^{i\kappa x} e^{-\frac{x^2}{2\sigma^2}} I_r(x) \quad (12)$$

by the kernel $K(x, x_0)$. This can be shown to yield (Torreão, 2007)

$$I_2(x) = e^{i(\kappa x + \psi)} e^{-\frac{x^2}{2\sigma^2}} I_r(x - u) \quad (13)$$

where $I_r(x - u)$ is given by Eq. (7), for $u = \sigma^2/a$, and where $\psi = \kappa u$. Thus, filtering signal $I_1(x)$ by the kernel $K(x, x_0)$ essentially preserves its Gabor modulating factor (with the introduction of a phase), but spatially shifts the modulated image.

Assuming that, locally – *i.e.*, under the Gaussian window of the Gabor modulating function –, the disparity between the right and left input images is well approximated by u, such that $I_l(x) \approx I_r(x - u)$, we would be able to rewrite Eq. (13) as

$$I_2(x) = e^{i(\kappa x + \psi)} e^{-\frac{x^2}{2\sigma^2}} I_l(x) \quad (14)$$

Together with Eq. (12), this would then mean that $I_1(x)$ and $I_2(x)$ correspond, respectively, to a right and a left stereo images, as seen through the receptive fields of a quadrature pair of simple cortical cells, according to the so-called *phase-shift* model of stereo responses (Fleet et al., 1991).

Thus, operating on the equivalent to the *right-eye* cortical input (*viz.*, the right-eye *retinal* image as seen through the simple cell right-eye receptive field), the Green's kernel $K(x, x_0)$ produces the equivalent to the *left-eye* cortical input (*viz.*, the left-eye *retinal* image as seen through the simple cell left-eye receptive field).

If we change right for left and left for right in the foregoing development, it also becomes valid for the Green's kernel $K^{(-)}(x, x_0)$. Namely, being

$$I_1^{(-)}(x) = e^{i\kappa x} e^{-\frac{x^2}{2\sigma^2}} I_l(x) \tag{15}$$

the Gabor-modulated signal to be filtered by $K^{(-)}(x, x_0)$, we obtain

$$I_2^{(-)}(x) = e^{i(\kappa x - \psi)} e^{-\frac{x^2}{2\sigma^2}} I_l(x + u) \tag{16}$$

where, once again, $u = \sigma^2/a$. And Eq. (16) can also be rewritten, similarly to Eq. (14), as

$$I_2^{(-)}(x) = e^{i(\kappa x - \psi)} e^{-\frac{x^2}{2\sigma^2}} I_r(x) \tag{17}$$

Thus, operating on the equivalent to the *left-eye* cortical input (*viz.*, the left-eye *retinal* image as seen through the simple cell left-eye receptive field), the Green's kernel $K^{(-)}(x, x_0)$ produces the equivalent to the *right-eye* cortical input (*viz.*, the right-eye *retinal* image as seen through the simple cell right-eye receptive field).

Therefore, if we now compute the local match between the signals $I_2(x)$ and $I_2^{(-)}(x)$ – for instance, through the measure

$$R(x) = |I_2(x) - I_2^{(-)}(x)|^2 \tag{18}$$

– we will be effectively assessing the match between a left- and a right- cortical images, under the assumption that the local disparity is $2u$ (recall Eqs. (13) and (16)). Different u values can be obtained by changing the parameter a of the Green's kernels, while keeping σ and κ fixed, as proposed in (Torreão, 2007). This allows the estimation of the local disparity, for instance, as

$$d(x) = \frac{2\sigma^2}{\bar{a}(x)} \tag{19}$$

where $\bar{a}$ is that a value for which the measure $R(x)$ is minimized.

Incidentally, the measure $R(x)$ affords the comparison of the Green's function approach with the energy model for disparity estimation (Qian, 1994; Qian & Miakelian, 2000). Using Eqs. (13) and (16), we can rewrite it as

$$R(x) = e^{\frac{-x^2}{\sigma^2}} |I_r(x - u) - e^{i\Delta\psi} I_l(x + u)|^2 \tag{20}$$

where $\Delta\psi = -2\kappa u$. When considered for $x = 0$, Eq. (20), apart from the minus sign in front of the phase factor (which can be easily accomodated by assuming a phase difference of π between the Gabor modulating functions in Eqs. (12) and (15)), is similar to what is predicted for the complex cell response, by the *phase-and-position-shift* energy model. In the present case, the position shift is given by the disparity measure, $d = 2u$, and the phase shift, by $\Delta\psi$.

3. Stimulus-dependent receptive fields

The receptive field (RF) of a visual neuron defines the portion of the visible world where light stimuli evoke the neuron's response, and describes the nature of such response, distinguishing, for instance, excitatory and inhibitory subfields (Hubel & Wiesel, 1962). In the standard description, the spatial organization of the RF remains invariant, and the neuronal response is obtained by filtering the input through a fixed receptive field function. Lately, this classical view has been challenged by neurophysiological experiments which indicate that the receptive field organization changes with the stimuli (Allman et al., 1985; Bair, 2005; David et al., 2004). Motivated by such findings, we have proposed a model for stimulus-dependent receptive field functions – initially for cortical simple cells (Torreão et al., 2009), and later for center-surround (CS) structures, such as found in the retina and in the lateral geniculate nucleus (Torreão & Victer, 2010). In what follows, we present a brief description of the model as originally proposed for simple cells – which is mathematically easier to handle –, later extending it to the CS structures.

3.1 Cortical receptive fields

Let us first consider a one-dimensional model. Being $I(x)$ any square-integrable signal, it can be expressed as

$$I(x) = \int_{-\infty}^{\infty} e^{i[\omega x+\varphi(\omega)]} e^{-\frac{x^2}{2\sigma^2(\omega)}} * e^{i\omega x} d\omega \tag{21}$$

where the aterisk denotes a spatial convolution, and where $\sigma(\omega)$ and $\varphi(\omega)$ are related, respectively, to the magnitude and the phase of the signal's Fourier transform, $\tilde{I}(\omega)$, as

$$\tilde{I}(\omega) = (2\pi)^{3/2}\sigma(\omega)e^{i\varphi(\omega)} = \int_{-\infty}^{\infty} e^{-i\omega x} I(x)dx \tag{22}$$

Eq. (21) can be verified by rewriting the integral on its right-hand side in terms of the variable ω', and taking the Fourier transform (FT) of both sides. Using the linearity of the FT, and the property of the transform of a convolution, we obtain

$$\tilde{I}(\omega) = (2\pi)^{3/2} \int_{-\infty}^{\infty} \sigma(\omega')e^{i\varphi(\omega')}e^{-\frac{\sigma^2}{2}(\omega-\omega')^2}\delta(\omega-\omega')d\omega' \tag{23}$$

and, by making use of the sampling property of the delta,

$$\tilde{I}(\omega) = (2\pi)^{3/2}\sigma(\omega)e^{i\varphi(\omega)} \tag{24}$$

which is exactly the definition in Eq. (22).
Also, if we make the convolution operation explicit in Eq. (21), it can be formally rewritten as

$$I(x) = \int_{-\infty}^{\infty} < e^{i[\omega x+\varphi(\omega)]} e^{-\frac{x^2}{2\sigma^2(\omega)}}, e^{i\omega x} > e^{i\omega x} d\omega \tag{25}$$

where the angle brackets denote an inner product,

$$< f(x), g(x) >= \int_{-\infty}^{\infty} f(x)g^*(x)dx \tag{26}$$

with $g^*(x)$ standing for the complex conjugate of $g(x)$. Comparing Eq. (25) to a signal expansion on the Fourier basis set,

$$I(x) = \int_{-\infty}^{\infty} < I(x), e^{i\omega x} > e^{i\omega x} d\omega \tag{27}$$

we conclude that, in so far as the frequency ω is concerned, the Gabor function

$$e^{i[\omega x+\varphi(\omega)]}e^{-\frac{x^2}{2\sigma^2(\omega)}} \tag{28}$$

is equivalent to the signal $I(x)$. Thus, we have found a set of signal-dependent functions, localized in space and in frequency, which yield an exact representation of the signal, under the form

$$I(x) = \int_{-\infty}^{\infty}\int_{-\infty}^{\infty} e^{i[\omega x+\varphi(\omega)]}e^{-\frac{(x-\xi)^2}{2\sigma^2(\omega)}}d\xi d\omega \tag{29}$$

which amounts to a Gabor expansion with unit coefficients (the above result can be easily verified, again by making the spatial convolution explicit in Eq. (21)).
In (Torreão et al., 2009), the above development has been extended to two dimensions, and proposed as a model for image representation by cortical simple cells, whose receptive fields are well described by Gabor functions (Marcelja, 1980). In the 2D case, Eq. (21) becomes

$$I(x,y) = \int_{-\infty}^{\infty}\int_{-\infty}^{\infty} \psi_c(x,y;\omega_x,\omega_y) * e^{i(\omega_x x+\omega_y y)}d\omega_x d\omega_y \tag{30}$$

where

$$\psi_c(x,y;\omega_x,\omega_y) = e^{i[\omega_x x+\omega_y y+\varphi(\omega_x,\omega_y)]}e^{-\frac{(x^2+y^2)}{2\sigma_c^2(\omega_x,\omega_y)}} \tag{31}$$

is the model receptive field, with $\varphi(\omega_x,\omega_y)$ being the phase of the image's Fourier transform, and with $\sigma_c(\omega_x,\omega_y)$ being related to its magnitude, as

$$\sigma_c(\omega_x,\omega_y) = \frac{1}{(2\pi)^{3/2}}\sqrt{|\tilde{I}(\omega_x,\omega_y)|} \tag{32}$$

The validity of Eq. (30) can be ascertained similarly as in the one-dimensional case. Moreover, as shown in (Torreão et al., 2009), the same expansion also holds with good approximation over finite windows, with different σ_c and φ values computed locally at each window. Under such approximation, it makes sense to take the coding functions $\psi_c(x,y;\omega_x,\omega_y)$ as models for signal-dependent, Gabor-like receptive fields.

3.2 Center-surround receptive fields

A similar approach can be followed for neurons with center-surround organization, as presented in (Torreão & Victer, 2010). The role of the center-surround receptive fields – as found in the retina and in the lateral geniculate nucleus (LGN) – has been described as that of relaying decorrelated versions of the input images to the higher areas of the visual pathway (Attick & Redlich, 1992; Dan et al., 1996). The retina- and LGN-cells would thus have developed receptive field structures ideally suited to whiten natural images, whose spectra are known to decay, approximately, as the inverse of the frequency magnitude – *i.e.*, $\sim (\omega_x^2+\omega_y^2)^{-1/2}$ (Ruderman & Bialek, 1994). In accordance with such interpretation, we have introduced circularly symmetrical coding functions which yield a similar representation as Eq. (30) for a whitened image, and which have been shown to account for the neurophysyiological properties of center-surround cells.

Specifically, we have

$$I_{white}(x,y) = \int_{-\infty}^{\infty}\int_{-\infty}^{\infty} \psi(r;\omega_x,\omega_y) * e^{i(\omega_x x+\omega_y y)} d\omega_x d\omega_y \tag{33}$$

where $I_{white}(x,y)$ is a whitened image, and where $\psi(r;\omega_x,\omega_y)$ is the CS receptive field function, with $r = \sqrt{x^2+y^2}$. Following the usual approach (Attick & Redlich, 1992; Dan et al., 1996), we have modeled the whitened image as the result of convolving the input image with a zero-phase whitening filter,

$$I_{white}(x,y) = W(x,y) * I(x,y) \tag{34}$$

where $W(x,y)$ is such as to equalize the spectrum of natural images, at the same time suppressing high-frequency noise. The whitening filter spectrum has thus been chosen under the form

$$\tilde{W}(\omega_x,\omega_y) = \frac{\rho}{1+\kappa\rho^2} \tag{35}$$

where κ is a free parameter, and $\rho = \sqrt{\omega_x^2+\omega_y^2}$.

On the other hand, the signal-dependent receptive field has been taken under the form

$$\psi(r;\omega_x,\omega_y) = -\frac{e^{i\varphi(\omega_x,\omega_y)}}{\pi r}\left\{1-\cos[\sigma(\omega_x,\omega_y)\pi r]-\sin[\sigma(\omega_x,\omega_y)\pi r]\right\} \tag{36}$$

where φ is the phase of the Fourier transform of the input signal, as already defined, while $\sigma(\omega_x,\omega_y)$ is related to the magnitude of that transform, as

$$\sigma(\omega_x,\omega_y) = \frac{\rho}{\pi}\sqrt{1-\left[1+\frac{\rho\tilde{W}(\omega_x,\omega_y)|\tilde{I}(\omega_x,\omega_y)|}{4\pi}\right]^{-2}} \tag{37}$$

Eq. (37) can be verified by introducing the above $\psi(r;\omega_x,\omega_y)$ into Eq. (33), and taking the Fourier transform of both sides of that equation.

We remark that the most commonly used model of center-surround receptive fields, the difference of Gaussians (Enroth-Cugell et al., 1983), has not been considered in the above treatment, since it would have required two parameters for the definition of the coding functions, while our approach provides a single equation for this purpose.

Fig. 1 shows plots of the coding functions obtained from a 3×3 fragment of a natural image, for different frequencies. The figure displays the magnitude of $\psi(r;\omega_x,\omega_y)$ divided by σ, such that all functions reach the same maximum of 1, at $r = 0$. Each coding function displays a single dominant surround, whose size depends on the spectral content of the coded image at that particular frequency (when the phase factor in Eq. (36) is considered, we obtain both center-on and center-off organizations). For $\rho = 0$, σ vanishes, and the coding function becomes identically zero, meaning that the proposed model does not code uniform inputs. At low frequencies, the surround is well defined (Fig. 1a), becoming less so as the frequency increases (Fig. 1b), and all but disappearing at the higher frequencies (Fig. 1c). All such

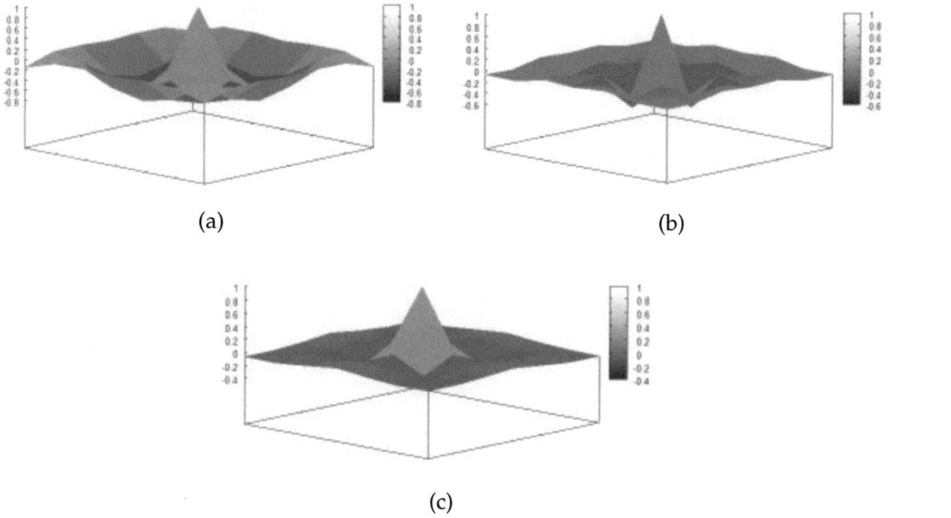

Fig. 1. Plots of the magnitude of the coding functions of Eq. (36), obtained from a 3×3 fragment of a natural image. The represented frequencies, (ω_x, ω_y), in (a), (b) and (c), are (0,1), (2,0), and (3,1), respectively.

properties are consistent with the behavior of retinal ganglion cells, or of cells of the lateral geniculate nucleus.

Fig. 2 shows examples of image coding by the signal-dependent CS receptive fields. The whitened representation is obtained, for each input, by computing Eq. (33) over finite windows. As shown by the log-log spectra in the figure (the vertical axis plots the rotational average of the log magnitude of the signal's FT, and the horizontal axis is $\log \rho$), the approach tends to equalize the middle portion of the original spectra, yielding representations similar to edge maps which code both edge strength and edge polarity. We have observed that the effect of the κ parameter in Eq. (35) is not pronounced, but, consistent with its role as a noise measure, larger κ values usually tend to enhance the low frequencies.

In the following section, we will use the whitened representation of stereo image pairs as input to the Green's function algorithm of Section 2, showing that this allows improved disparity estimation through an approach which is closer to the neurophysiological situation.

4. Green's function stereo with whitened inputs

We have incorporated a whitening routine into the stereo matching algorithm of Section 2, such that the Green's function procedure is now performed over signals which emulate the neurocortical input from the lower visual areas. Thus, what we have identified as *retinal* images, in Section 2.3, become the whitened representations of the stereo pair, obtained, through Eq. (33), by means of center-surround, signal-dependent receptive field functions. Disparity estimation proceeds as described, with the proviso that, similarly as in (Torreão, 2007), instead of choosing precisely that disparity which minimizes the matching measure $R(x)$ (Eq. (18)), we take, as our estimate, the sum of all disparities considered, each weighted by the inverse of the corresponding $R(x)$ value. This yields a dense disparity map, avoiding the need of interpolation. The preprocessing alignment of the stereo pair, through

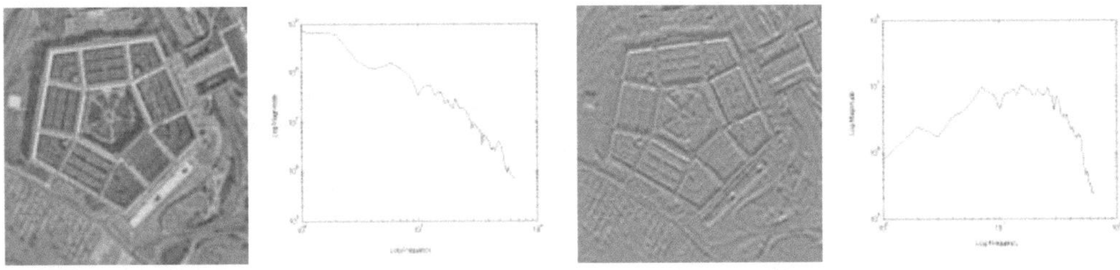

(a)

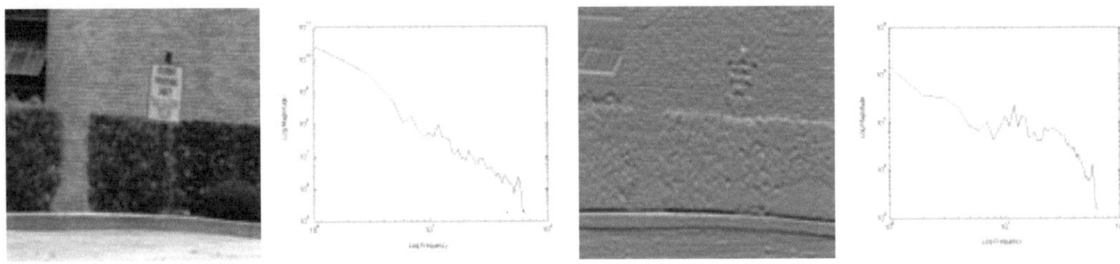

(b)

Fig. 2. a) Left: input image and its log-log spectrum. Right: whitened image and its log-log spectrum. Similarly for b). We have used 3×3 windows, with $\kappa = 0.05$.

uniform-disparity matching, has also been followed (Torreão, 2007), as a means for handling large overall disparities.

Figs. 3 to 6 depict some results of the whitened Green's function stereo, along with those yielded by the original approach. It is apparent that the former generally affords better spatial resolution, as well as sharper disparity definition. Being based on whitened inputs, the new algorithm proves less sensitive to image features not depth related, as can be seen in the background region of the meter stereo pair (Fig. 6), more uniformly captured by the whitened approach than by the original one, which is biased by the complex edge structure in the region.

5. Conclusion

In this chapter, we have reviewed the Green's function stereoscopy (Torreão, 2007) – a neurophyisiologically-inspired stereo matching approach –, along with a recently introduced model for signal-dependent receptive fields (Torreão et al., 2009; Torreão & Victer, 2010). By coupling the Green's function algorithm with a whitening representation of the stereo inputs, based on center-surround, signal-dependent receptive field functions, we have been able to obtain better disparity estimates, through an approach which is closer to the neurophysiological situation. We are presently working on the incorporation, into our stereo algorithm, of the Gabor-like, signal-dependent receptive model of Section 3.1. This will allow a more realistic parallel with the cortical mechanisms of biological stereo vision.

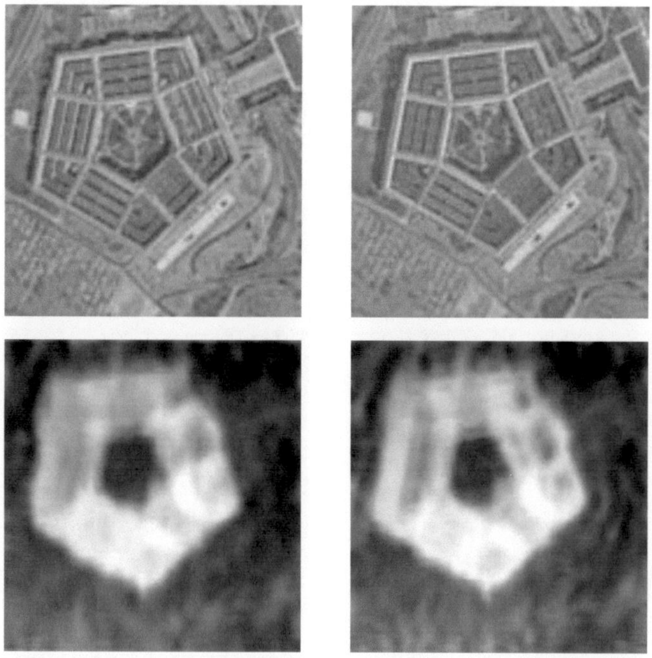

Fig. 3. Top: Pentagon stereo pair. Bottom: Disparity maps obtained through the whitened Green's function approach (left) and through the original approach of (Torreão, 2007) (right).

Fig. 4. Top: Tree stereo pair. Bottom: Disparity maps obtained through the whitened Green's function approach (left) and through the original approach of (Torreão, 2007) (right).

Fig. 5. Top: Shrub stereo pair. Bottom: Disparity maps obtained through the whitened Green's function approach (left) and through the original approach of (Torreão, 2007) (right).

Fig. 6. Top: Meter stereo pair. Bottom: Disparity maps obtained through the whitened Green's function approach (left) and through the original approach of (Torreão, 2007) (right).

6. References

Adelson, E.H. & Bergen, J.R. (1985). Spatiotemporal energy models for the perception of motion. J. Opt. Soc. Am. A 2, pp. 284–299.

Allman, J.; Miezin, F. & McGuinness, E. (1985). Stimulus specific responses from beyond the classical receptive field: Neurophysiological mechanisms for local-global comparison in visual neurons. Annu. Rev. Neuroscience 8, pp. 407–430.

Atick, J.J. & Redlich, A.N. (1992). What does the retina know about natural scenes? Neural Comp. 4, pp. 196–210.

Bair,W. (2005). Visual receptive field organization. Current Opinion in Neurobiology 15(4), pp. 459–464.

Chen, Y. & Qian, N. (2004). A coarse-to-fine disparity energy model with both phase-shift and position-shift receptive field mechanisms. Neural Comput. 16, pp. 1545–1577.

Dan, Y., Atick, J.J. & Reid, R.C. (1996). Efficient coding of natural scenes in the lateral geniculate nucleus: experimental test of a computational theory. J. Neurosci. 16(10), pp. 3351–3362.

David, S.V.; Vinje, W.E. & Gallant, J.L. (2004). Natural stimulus statistics alter the receptive field structure of V1 neurons, The Journal of Neuroscience 24(31), pp. 6991–7006.

Enroth-Cugell, C.; Robson, J.G.; Schweitzer-Tong, D.E., & Watson, A.B. (1983). Spatiotemporal interactions in cat retinal ganglion cells showing linear spatial summation, J. Physiol. 341, pp. 279–301.

Fleet, D.J.; Jepson, A.D. & Jenkin, M.R.M. (1991). Phase-based disparity measurement. Comp. Vis. Graphics Image Proc. 53(2), pp. 198–210.

Hubel, D.H. & Wiesel, T. (1962). Receptive fields, binocular interaction and functional architecture in the cat's visual cortex. J. Physiol. 160, pp. 106–154.

Marcelja, S. (1980). Mathematical description of the responses of simple cortical cells. J. Opt. Soc. Am. A 70, pp. 1297–1300.

Ohzawa, I.; DeAngelis, J.C. & Freeman, R.D. (1997). Encoding of binocular disparity by complex cells in the cat's visual cortex. J. Neurophysiol. 77(6), pp. 2879–2909.

Qian, N. (1994). Computing stereo disparity and motion with known binocular cell properties. Neural Comput. 6, pp. 390–404.

Qian, N. & Mikaelian, S. (2000). Relationship between phase and energy methods for disparity computation. Neural Comput. 12, pp. 303–316.

Ruderman, D.L. & Bialek, W. (1994). Statistics of natural images: Scaling in the woods, Phys. Rev. Lett. 73(6), pp. 814–817.

Torreão, J.R.A. (2007). Disparity estimation through Green's functions of matching equations. Biol. Cybernetics 97, pp. 307–316.

Torreão, J.R.A.; Fernandes, J.L.; Amaral M.S. & Beltrão, L. (2007). Green's functions of matching equations: A unifying approach for low-level vision problems In: *Vision Systems: Segmentation and Pattern Recognition*, G. Obinatta and A. Dutta, pp. 381-396, I-Tech Education and Publishing, ISBN 978-3-902613-05-9, Vienna, Austria.

Torreão, J.R.A.; Fernandes, J.L. & Victer, S.M.C. (2009). A model for neuronal signal representation by stimulus-dependent receptive fields, *Proceedings of the 19th International Conference on Artificial Neural Networks - ICANN 2009*, Limassol, Cyprus, Springer, vol. I, pp. 356–362.

Torreão, J.R.A. & Victer, S.M.C. (2010). A model for center-surround stimulus dependent receptive fields, *Proceedings of the 20th International Conference on Artificial Neural Networks - ICANN 2010*, Thessaloniki, Greece, Springer, vol. I, pp. 305–310.

5

High-Speed Architecture Based on FPGA for a Stereo-Vision Algorithm

M.-A. Ibarra-Manzano[1] and D.-L. Almanza-Ojeda[2]

[1]*Digital Signal Processing Laboratory, Electronics Department; DICIS*
University of Guanajuato
[2]*Mechatronic Department, Campus Loma Bonita*
University of Papaloapan
[1]*Salamanca, Guanajuato, Mexico*
[2]*Loma Bonita, Oaxaca, Mexico*

1. Introduction

Stereo vision is used to reconstruct the 3D (depth) information of a scene from two images, called left and right. This information is acquired from two cameras separated by a previously established distance. Stereo vision is a very popular technique used for applications such as mobile robotics, autoguided vehicles and 3D model acquisition. However, the real-time performance of these applications cannot be achieved by conventional computers, because the processing is computationally expensive. For this reason, other solutions like reconfigurable architectures have been proposed to execute dense computational algorithms.

In the last decade, several works have proposed the development of high-performance architectures to solve the stereo-vision problem i.e. digital signal processing (DSP), field programmable gate arrays (FPGA) or application-specific integrated circuits (ASIC). The ASIC devices are one of the most complicated and expensive solutions, however they afford the best condition for developing a final commercial system (Woodfill et al., 2006). On the other hand, FPGA have allowed the creation of hardware designs in standard, high-volume parts, thereby amortizing the cost of mask sets and significantly reducing time-to-market for hardware solutions. However, engineering cost and design time for FPGA-based solutions still remain significantly higher than software-based solutions. Designers must frequently iterate the design process in order to achieve system performance requirements and simultaneously minimize the required size of the FPGA. Each iteration of this process takes hours or days to be completed (Schmit et al., 2000). Even if designing with FPGAs is faster than designing ASICs, it has a finite resource capacity which demands clever strategies for adapting versatile real-time systems (Masrani & MacLean, 2006).

In this chapter, we present a high-speed reconfigurable architecture of the Census Transform algorithm (Zabih & Woodfill, 1994) for calculating the disparity map from a dense stereo-vision system. The reuse of operations and the integer/binary nature of these operations were carefully adapted on the FPGA for obtaining a final architecture that generates up to 325 dense disparity maps of 640×480 pixels, even though most of the vision-based systems do not require high video-frame rates. In this context, we propose a stereo-vision system that can be adapted to the real-time application requirements. An analysis of the four essential architectural parameters (such as the size of the window of the arithmetic mean and median filters, the maximal disparity and the window size for the Census Transform), is carried out to obtain the best trade off between consumed resources and the disparity map accuracy. We vary these parameters and show a graphical representation of the consumed resources versus the desired performance for different extended architectures. From these curves, we can easily select the most appropriate architecture for our application. Furthermore, we develop a practical application of the obtained disparity map to tackle the problem of 3D environment reconstruction using the back-projection technique. Experimental performance results are compared to those of related architectures.

2. Overview of passive stereo vision

In computer vision, stereo vision intends to recover depth information from two images of the same scene. A pixel in one image corresponds to a pixel in the other, if both pixels are projections of the same physical scene element. Also, if the two images are spatially separated but simultaneous, then computing correspondence determines stereo depth (Zabih & Woodfill, 1994). There are two main approaches to process the stereo correlation: feature-based and area-based. In this work, we are more interested in area-based approaches, because they propose a dense solution for calculating high-density disparity maps. Furthermore, these approaches have a regular algorithmic structure which is suitable for a convenient hardware architecture. The global dense stereo vision algorithm used in this work is based on the Census Transform. This algorithm was first introduced by Zabih and Woodfill (Zabih & Woodfill, 1994). Figure 1 shows the block diagram of the global algorithm.

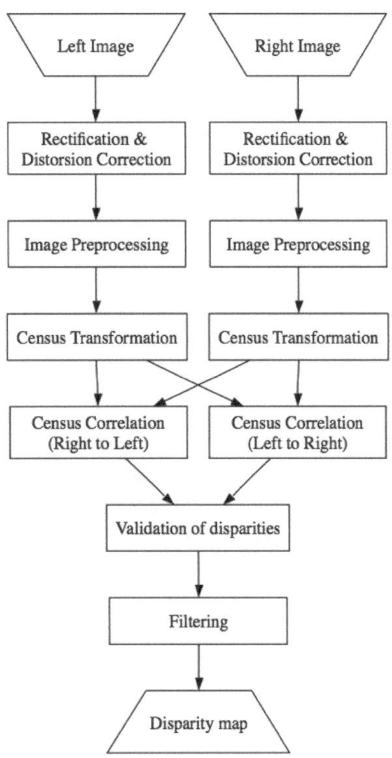

Fig. 1. Stereo vision algorithm

First of all, the algorithm processes in parallel and independently each of the images (right and left). The process begins with the rectification and correction of the distortion for each image. This process allows us to reduce the size of the search of points for the calculation of the disparity to a single dimension. In order to reduce the complexity and size of the required architecture, this algorithm uses the epipolar restriction. In this restriction, the main axes of the cameras should be aligned in parallel, so that the epipolar lines between the two cameras correspond to the displacement of the position between the two pixels (one per camera). Under this condition, an object location in the scene is reduced to a horizontal translation. If any pair of pixels is visible in both cameras and assuming they are the projection of a single point in the scene, then both pixels must be aligned on the same epipolar line (Ibarra-Manzano, Almanza-Ojeda, Devy, Boizard & Fourniols, 2009).

2.1 Image preprocessing

The Census Transform requires that left and right input images be pre-processed. During image pre-processing, we use an arithmetic mean filter that requires a rectangular window of size $m \times n$ pixels. S_{uv} represents a set of image coordinates inside of the rectangular window centered on the point (u, v). The arithmetic mean filter calculates the mean value in the noisy image $I(u, v)$ at each rectangular window defined by S_{uv}. The corrected image value $\hat{I}$ takes this arithmetic mean value at each point (u, v) of subset S_{uv} (see Equation 1).

$$\hat{I}(u,v) = \frac{1}{m \times n} \sum_{(i,j) \in S_{uv}} I(i,j) \tag{1}$$

This filter could be implemented without using the scale factor $1/(m \times n)$ because the size of the window is constant during the filtering process. The arithmetic mean filter smooths local variations in the image, at the same time, the noise produced by camera motions is notably reduced.

2.2 Census Transform

Once input images have been filtered, they are used to calculate the Census Transform. This transform is a non-parametric measure used during the matching process for measuring similarities and obtaining the correspondence between the points into the left and right images. A neighborhood of pixels is used for establishing the relationships among them (see Equation 2),

$$I_C(u,v) = \bigotimes_{(i,j) \in D_{uv}} \xi\left(\hat{I}(u,v), \hat{I}(i,j)\right) \tag{2}$$

where D_{uv} represents the set of coordinates into the square window of size $n \times n$ pixels (being n an odd number) and centered at the point (u, v). The function ξ is the comparison of the intensity level among the center pixel (u, v) with all the pixels in D_{uv}. This function returns '1' if the intensity of the pixel (i, j) is lower than the intensity of the centering pixel (u, v), otherwise the function returns '0'. The operator $\otimes$ represents the concatenation function among each bit calculated by the function ξ. I_C represents the Census Transform of the point (u, v) which is a bit chain.

2.3 Census correlation

The two pixels (one for each image) obtained from the Census Transform are compared using the Hamming distance. This comparison which is called the correlation process allows us to obtain a disparity measure. The similarity evaluation is based on the binary comparison between two bit chains given by the Census Transform. The disparity measure from left to right D_{H1} in the point (u,v) is calculated by the equation 3, where I_{Cl} and I_{Cr} represent the left and right images of the Census Transform, respectively. This disparity measure comes from the similarity maximization function in the same epipolar line v for the two images. In this same equation, D represents the maximal displacement value on the epipolar line of the right image. The function $\bar{\otimes}$ represents the binary operator $XNOR$.

$$D_{H1}(u,v) = \max_{d\in[0,D]} \left(\frac{1}{N} \sum_{i=1}^{N} I_{Cl}(u,v)_i \,\bar{\otimes} I_{Cr}(u-d,v)_i \right) \tag{3}$$

The correlation process is carried out two times, (left to right then right to left) with the aim of reducing the disparity error. The equation 4 is for that case in which the right to left disparity measure is calculated. This measure was added for complementing the process. Contrary to the previous disparity measure shown in equation 3, the equation 4 uses the following pixels with respect to the current pixel in the search process.

$$D_{H2}(u,v) = \max_{d\in[0,D]} \left(\frac{1}{N} \sum_{i=1}^{N} I_{Cl}(u+d,v)_i \,\bar{\otimes} I_{Cr}(u,v)_i \right) \tag{4}$$

2.4 Disparity validation

Once both disparity measures have been obtained, the validating task is straightforward. The disparity measure validation (right to left and left to right) consists of comparing both disparity values and obtaining the absolute difference between them. In the case that this difference is lower than a predefined threshold δ, then the disparity value is accepted. Otherwise, the disparity value is labeled as undefined. The equation 5 represents the validation of the disparity measures, D_H being the validation result.

$$D_H = \begin{cases} D_{H1} & |D_{H1} - D_{H2}| < \delta \\ ind & |D_{H1} - D_{H2}| \geq \delta \end{cases} \tag{5}$$

2.5 Disparity filtering

A novel filtering process is needed in order to improve the quality of the final disparity image. M_{uv} is the set of coordinates in a $m \times n$ rectangular window centered on the point (u,v). First, the set of disparity values $D_H(i,j)$ in the region defined by M_{uv} are ordered. After that, the median filtering process selects the centered value at the ordered list. This value is set into the region defined by an $M \times N$ rectangular window $M_{u,v}$ and the same process is carried out for all the image pixels (i,j) in order to obtain the filtered image $\tilde{D}_H$. Hence, this filtered image calculated by the median filter, when expressed in terms of the central pixel (u,v), would be written as in equation 6.

$$\tilde{D}_H(u,v) = \text{median}\left(D_H(i,j), (i,j) \in M_{uv}\right) \tag{6}$$

Whereas, for the image preprocessing (described above), an arithmetic mean filter is used, here for the pre-filtering process a median spatial filter is used, because the median filter allows the selection of one value among all the disparity values for representing the disparity in the search window. This means that a new value does not need to be obtained, as in the arithmetic filter.

3. Hardware implementation

We have implemented an architecture for FPGA that implements several image processing tasks with high performance. During the architecture design, we try to minimize the consumed resources in the FPGA for maximizing the system performance. In previous subsections, we have explained the 4 essential tasks of our architecture: the image processing, the Census Transform, the disparity validation and the filtering of the disparity image. In this section, we describe the hardware implementation, that is, how these architectures are implemented into the FPGA.

3.1 The arithmetic mean filter module

Usually the image acquired from the camera is not so noisy, thus a fast smoothing function could be used for obtaining a good quality image. For this reason, we use the arithmetic mean filter, which is faster and easy to implement. We are often interested in the minimization of required resources, so that, after several tests, we choose a window size of 3×3 pixels that is also enough for achieving good results. Indeed, this size allows us to save resources in the final architecture.

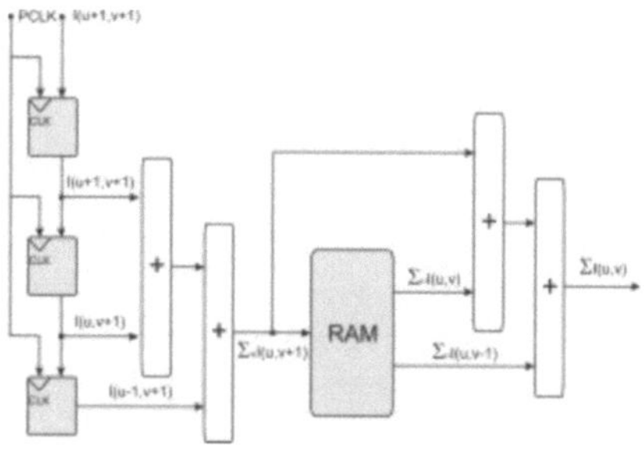

Fig. 2. Module architecture to calculate the arithmetic mean filter.

The arithmetic mean calculation is carried out in two stages: in horizontal and vertical ways. The block diagram of this architecture, in accordance with the process described in subsection 2.1, is shown in figure 2. The three input registers (left side of the diagram) are used for the horizontal addition. These registers are connected to two 8-bit parallel adders, although the result is coded in 10 bits. The result of this operation is stored in the memory that is twice the length image size. For obtaining the sum of all the elements in the window, a vertical addition is carried out. This addition uses the current horizontal addition result plus the two previous horizontal additions stored in the memory. This is shown on the right side of the diagram. Finally the arithmetic mean of the nine pixels are codified in a 12 bit-chain. In this stage, the delay only depends on the operation that involves the last line plus one value.

3.2 The Census Transform module

The arithmetic mean of the left and right images are used as inputs in the Census Transform stage. This transformation codifies all the intensity values inside the search window with respect to the central intensity value.

The block diagram of the Census Transform architecture is shown in the figure 3. The performance in this module depends on the size of the search window. The size of this window directly increases the resources and the time of processing. So the best trade off between the consumed resources and the optimal size of the window has to be selected. After several tests, the best processing time and hardware saving resources is reached for a 7×7

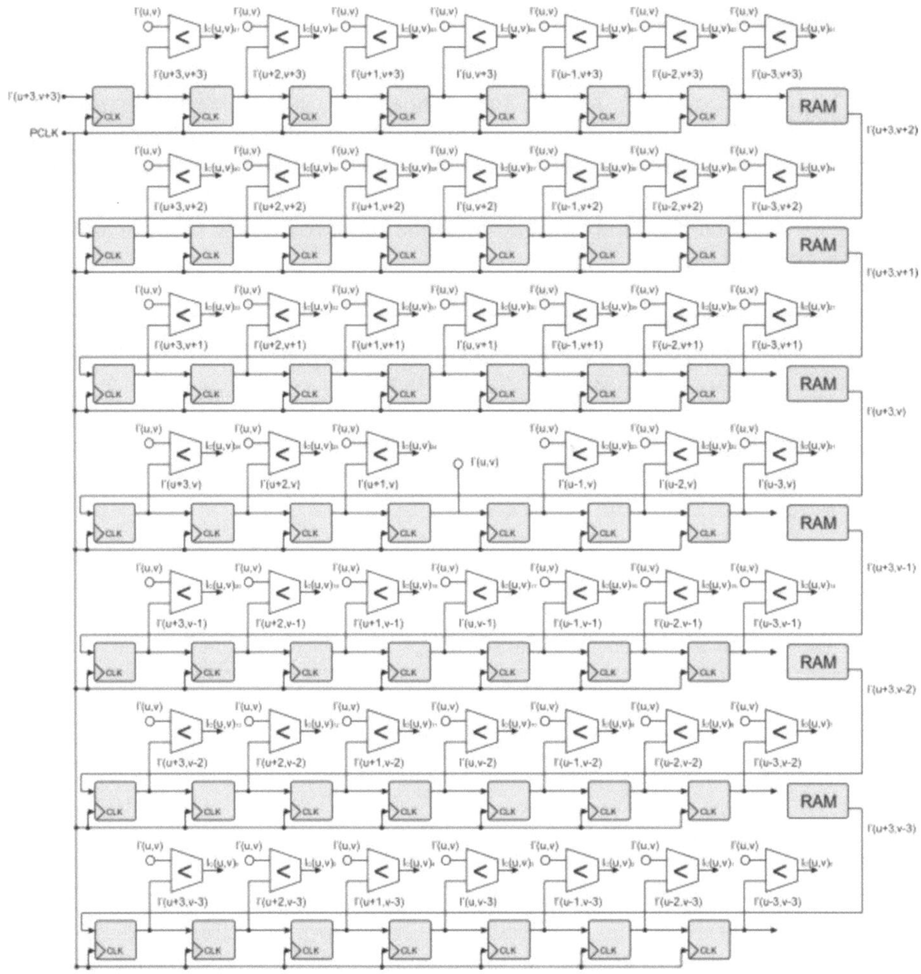

Fig. 3. Module architecture to calculate the Census Transform.

pixels window. This window needs 49 registers. On the other hand, 6 memory blocks are used in the processing module. The size of these memory blocks is obtained as follows: size of the image (usually 640) minus the size of the search window (7 pixels in our case) and the result is multiplied by 12. The constant 12 in the last multiplication is used because we look for the same size in the input of the Census Transform rather than in the output of the arithmetic mean module. Once we have selected the size of the search window, then we continue with the description of the Census Transform. The central pixel in the search window is compared with their 48 local neighbors. This last operation implies the connection of all the corresponding registers with parallel comparators as is shown in figure 3. The result is codified in 48 bits, where each bit corresponds to the comparator outputs. This stage has a delay equal to half of the search window by the length of the image.

3.3 The census correlation module

The correlation process consists of analyzing left and right images resulting from the Census Transform. Considering that both images contain a common object, the correlation process has the aim of finding the displacement between two projected pixels belonging to that common object in the images. Hence, as images are acquired from two different points of view (associated with the left and right camera positions) there will exist a noticeable difference between point positions belonging to the same object, such difference is referred to as the disparity. Usually, the correlation intends to maximize the similarity between two images in order to find the disparity. We also use this common method which consists of two main stages: the calculation of the similarity measure and the search for the maximal value. Figure 4 shows the block diagram of the corresponding architecture. We are interested in reducing the delay in the correlation process, therefore it is more convenient to compare one point of the left Census Transform image with the maximal number of points in the right one. Furthermore, the correlation process is executed twice in order to minimize the error during the correlation computation. We will consider 64 pixels as the maximal disparity value for each left and right Census Transform image. The registers represented by the gray blocks on the left of figure 4 store those pixels. The registers as well as the pixels of the left Census Transform image enter the binary operators *XNOR* to deliver a 48-bit chain at the output. The *XNOR* function is used to find the maximal and minimal similarity associated with the disparity values at the input. All such pixel values enter by pairs into the *XNOR* gates. If all the compared pixels are equal, then the *XNOR* output will be '1', which means maximal similarity. Otherwise, if pixels are different, then 0 will be the output of the *XNOR*, which is associated with a minimal similarity value.

Once the similarity has been calculated, we continue with the search of the highest disparity values between the 64 pixels compared in both correlation results, from left to right and right to left correlations, but independently. This task requires several selector units, each one with 4 inputs distributed as follows: 2 for the similarity values that will be compared and 2 for the indicators. The indicators are associated with the displacement between pixels in the left and right Census Transform. That is, if one pixel has the same position in both right and left Census Transform, then the indicator will be zero. Otherwise, the indicator will represent the number of pixels between pixel position in the left Census Transform with respect to the pixel in the right one. The block diagram of the architecture shown in figure 4 describes graphically the implementation of the maximization process. By examining this figure, we can highlight that the selector unit receives two similarity measures and two indicators as inputs. The elements inside of these units are a multiplexer and a comparator. The multiplexer receives the pixel with the highest similarity value, while the comparator receives two similarity values that come from the first stage. Hence the output of that comparison will be considered as the selector inputs of the multiplexer. Thus, the multiplexer output will be the similarity measure and its refereed index pixel. However, in order to obtain the pixel with the maximal similarity measure, six levels of comparison units are needed. These levels are organized in a pyramidal fashion. The lowest level corresponds to the first layer that carries out the selector unit task described above 32 times. As we ascend the pyramid levels, each level reduces by half the number of operators used with the previous level. The last level delivers the highest similarity value between the corresponding pixels in the left and right Census images. Whereas right to left image correlation stores left Census Transform pixels, which are compared with one pixel of the right Census image, for left to right image correlation the comparison is relative to one pixel of the left Census image. For this reason, a similar architecture is used for developing both correlation processes. All this stage (including both right to left and left to right processes) has a delay that depends on the number of layers in the selector units, which at the same time depends on the maximal disparity value that we are using. In our case, we establish maximal disparity value to 64, thus the number of layers is equal to 6.

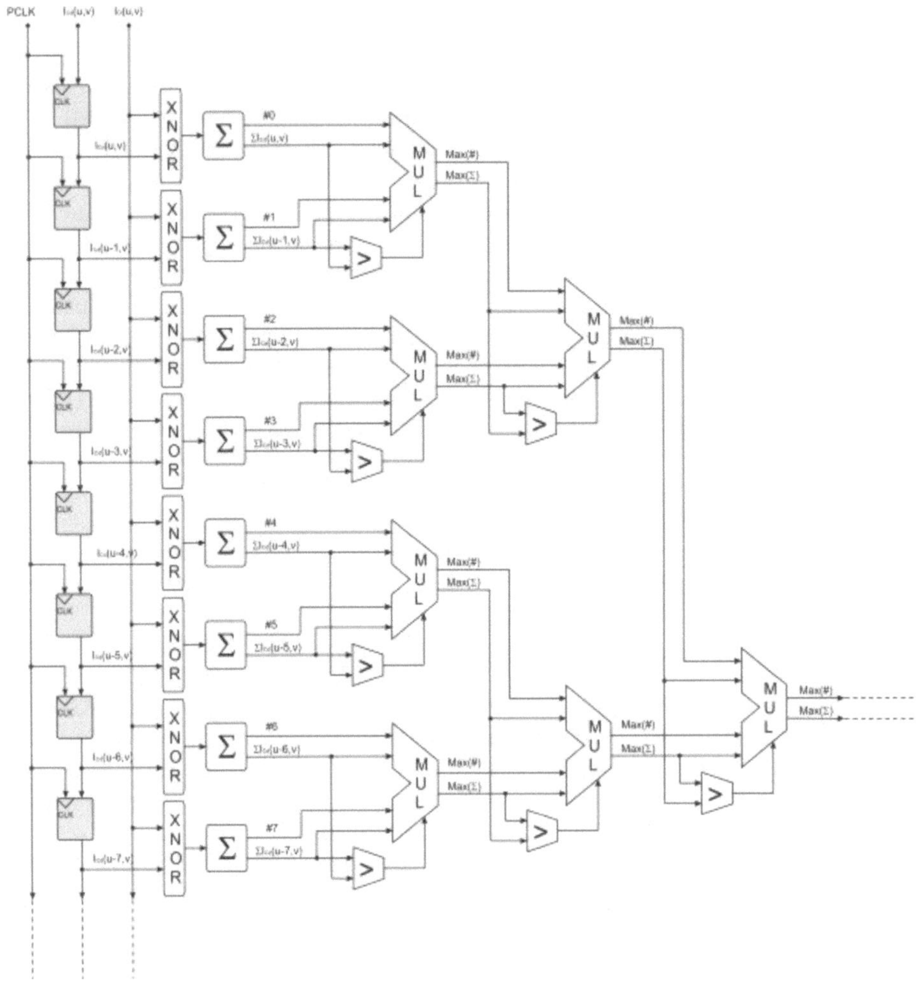

Fig. 4. Module architecture to calculate the Census correlation.

3.4 Disparity validation module

This module fuses the two disparity values obtained by the Census correlation processes (right to left and left to right). First, the difference between the two values is calculated, after that it is compared with a threshold δ. If that difference is lower than δ then the left to right disparity value is the output of the comparison, otherwise, the output will be labeled as undefined.

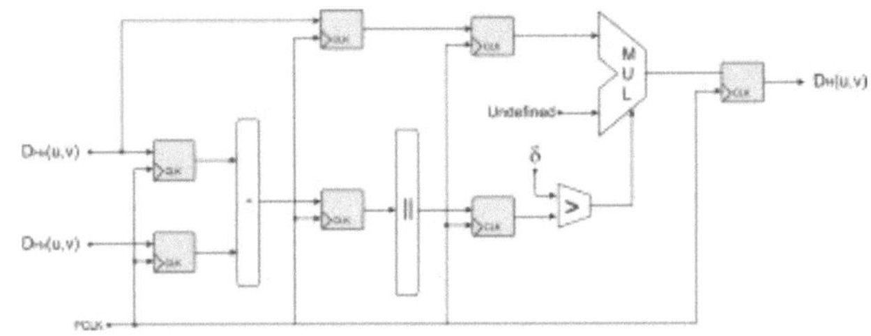

Fig. 5. Module architecture to validate the disparities.

The figure 5 shows the block diagram of the disparity validation architecture. The inputs of this module are the two disparity values obtained by the Census Correlation process. The absolute difference of values is used in the comparison with δ. The comparator delivers one bit that controls the multiplexer selector. If the result of the comparison is 1 (that is, δ is higher than the correlation differences), then the multiplexer will have the undefined label as result. This result is associated with the maximal disparity value plus one, which is referred to as the default value. If the comparison result is zero, then the output of the multiplexer will be the value of the left to right Census correlation.

3.5 The median filter module

Some errors have been detected during the disparity validation, due to the errors in the correlation process. Most of these errors appear because objects in the image have similar intensity values to their surrounding area. This situation produces very similar Census Transform values in pixels and consequently wrong disparity values in certain cases. We are interested in reducing these errors in the image by using a median filter. As we pointed out before, it is not recommended to use the same arithmetic mean filter as in the pre-processing stage because this filter will give us a new value (the average into the filtering window), which is not an element of the current disparity values. On the other hand the median filter works with the true values in the image, so the resulting value will be an element of the disparity window. The median filter uses a search window of size 3×3 pixels. This window is enough for notably reducing the error and improving the final disparity map as is shown in figure 6.

(a) Left stereo image (b) Disparity map (c) Filtered image of disparity map

Fig. 6. Median Filter. a) Left image, b) Resulting disparity map without filtering and c) with filtering.

Figure 7 shows the block diagram of the median filter architecture. This filter is based on the works of (Dhanasekaran & Bagan, 2009) and (Vega-Rodriguez et al., 2002). On the left side of the diagram is shown the nine registers and the two RAM block memories used to generate the sliding window that extracts the nine pixels of the processing window. This architecture works similar like to the processing window of the Census Transform. That is, the nine pixels in the window are processed by a pyramidal architecture but in this case with 9 levels. Each level contains several comparison units that find the higher value between two input values A and B. Each comparison unit contains a comparator and a multiplexer. If the input A in the comparator is higher than its input B, then the output will be 1, otherwise the output will be 0. The comparator output is used as a signal control of the multiplexer. When this signal is 1, then the multiplexer selects A as the higher value and B as the lower value, otherwise B is the higher value and A the lower one. Each comparator level in the median module orders the disparity values with respect to its neighbors in the processing window, completing in this way the descendent organization of all the values. However, here it is not necessary to order all the disparity values, because we are only looking for the middle value in the last level. Therefore, we only need the comparison unit at the last level, because previous levels give only the partial order of the elements. The connection structure between the comparison units at each level guaranty an optimal median value (Vega-Rodriguez et al., 2002).

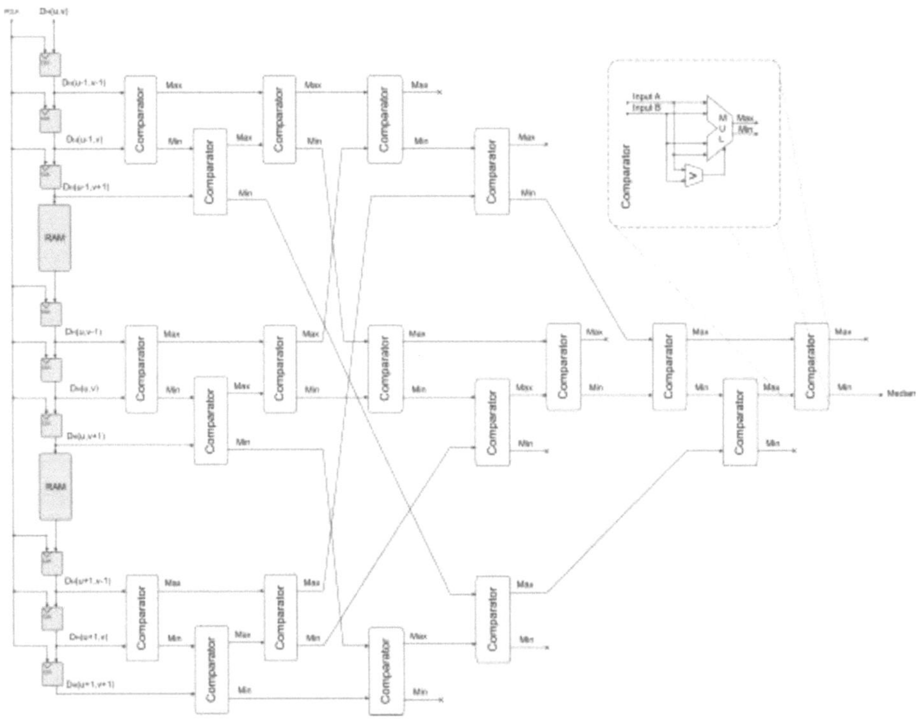

Fig. 7. Module architecture to calculate the median filter of disparities.

4. Resources and performance discussion

Our final architecture for executing the stereo vision algorithm based on the Census Transform was developed using the level design flow RTL (Ibarra-Manzano, 2011). The architecture was codified in VHDL language using Quartus II workspace and ModelSim. Finally, it was synthesized for an EP2C35F672C6 device contained in the Cyclone II family of Altera.
Some synthesis results associated with our architecture are: the implemented architecture implies 11,683 combinatorial functions and 5,162 dedicated logic registers, both represent 12,183 logic elements in total. The required memory is 112,025 bits. The quantity of logic elements represent only 37% of the total capacity in the device while the memory size represents 43%. The resources consumed by the architecture are directly associated with 5 essential parameters: the image size, window processing size used in both arithmetic mean and median filter, the window size in the search window of Census Transform and the maximal value in the disparity measure. In this architecture, we use an image size of 640×480 pixels, a window size of 3×3 pixels for both filters (arithmetic mean and median filters), a search window of 7×7 pixels for the Census Transform and a maximal disparity value of

64 pixels. With these parameters, the architecture is able to calculate 130 disparity images per second with a 50 Mhz signal clock until 325 disparity images per second with a 100 Mhz signal clock.

4.1 Architectural exploration through high-level synthesis

High level synthesis was used to implement the stereo vision architecture based on Census Transform. The algorithm was developed using GAUT (Coussy & Morawiec, 2008), which is a high level synthesis tool using C language. After that, the algorithm was synthesized using the (EP2C35F672C6) Cyclone II of Altera. Each state of the architecture (filtering, Census Transform and Correlation) was developed taking into account consumed resources and high performance (high speed of processing). The best trade off was found for implementing an optimal architecture system.
Tables 1 to 3 lay out three different architectures, labeled as Design 1, 2, and 3, with their most representative performance. In the following, we will describe how the different implementation details are related in our architecture. There exists a clear relation between performance, cadence and pipeline implementation. That is, if we reduce the performance, then the cadence increases, therefore the number of operations and stages in the pipeline is low. With the rest of feature design, it is more difficult to see how they are related. For example, the number of logic elements depends directly on the used combinational functions and the number of dedicated logic registers. The combinational functions are strongly associated with the quantity of operations and weakly with the state numbers in the state machine. As with any state machine, the cadence time controls the performance speed. Contrary to the combinational functions, the dedicated logic registers strongly depends on the number of states in the state machine and weakly on the number of operations. Finally, the delay is obtained based on the number of operations, the number of stages in the pipeline and specially in the cadence time established by the architecture design. The results shown in the tables 1 to 3 were carried out for an image size of 640×480 pixels with a processing window of 3×3 pixels for the arithmetic mean filter, a window size of 7×7 pixels for the Census Transform and a maximal disparity measure of 64 pixels, with a signal clock of 100 Mhz.

Characteristics	Design 1	Design 2	Design 3
Cadency (ns)	20	30	40
Performance (fps)	160	100	80
Logic elements	118	120	73
Comb, functions	86	72	73
Ded. log. registers	115	116	69
# Stages in pipeline	3	2	2
# Operators	2	2	1
Latency (μs)	25.69	38.52	51.35

Table 1. Comparative table for the arithmetic mean filter.

Taking into account the most common real time constraints, it is possible to choose the design 3 for the implementation of the arithmetic mean filter, because this represents the best compromise between performance and consumed resources. For the same reason, the design 2 could be chosen for developing the Census Transform and the design 3 for the Census correlation. The results of the hardware Synthesis in FPGA are summarized as follows: the global architecture needs 6,977 logic elements and 112,025 memory bits. The quantity of logic elements represents 21% of the total resources logic of the Cyclone II device, furthermore

Characteristics	Design 1	Design 2	Design 3
Cadency (ns)	40	80	200
Performance (fps)	80	40	15
Logic elements	2,623	1,532	1,540
Comb. functions	2,321	837	864
Ded. log. registers	2,343	1,279	1,380
# Stages in pipeline	48	24	10
# Operators	155	79	34
Latency (μs)	154.36	308.00	769.50

Table 2. Comparative table for the Census Transform.

Characteristics	Design 1	Design 2	Design 3
Cadency (ns)	20	40	80
Performance (fps)	160	80	40
Logic elements	1,693	2,079	2,644
Comb. functions	1,661	1,972	2,553
Ded. log. registers	1,369	1,451	1,866
# Stages in pipeline	27	12	8
# Operators	140	76	46
Latency (ns)	290	160	100

Table 3. Comparative table for the Census correlation.

the memory size represents 23%. This architecture calculates 40 dense disparity images per second with a clock of 100 Mhz. This performance is lower than the proposed architecture, although it proposes a well-optimized design, since it uses less resources than in the previous case. In spite of the low performance, this is high enough in the majority of real-time vision applications.

4.2 Comparative analysis of the architectures

First, we will analyze the system performance for four different solutions to the dense disparity image. Two of the above mentioned solutions are hardware implementations. The third one is a solution for a Digital Signal Processing (DSP) model ADSP-21161N, with a signal clock of 100 MHz from Analog Devices Company. The last one is a software solution for a PC DELL Optiplex 755 with a 2.00 Ghz Intel Core 2 Duo processor and 2 Gb in RAM. The performance comparison between these solutions is shown in table 4. The first column indicates the different image sizes used during the experimental test. The second column shows the sizes of the search window used in the Census Transform. The third column shows the processing time (performance).

In the FPGA implementation, the parallel processing allows short calculation time. The developed architecture uses the RTL level design which reaches the lower processing time, but it takes more time for the implementation. On the other hand, using high level synthesis for the architecture design allows the development of a less complex design, but it requires longer processing time. However, the advantage of high level synthesis is the short implementation time. Unlike FPGA implementations, the DSP solutions are easier and faster to implement, nevertheless the processing remains sequential, and so the computation time is considerably high. Finally, the PC solution, that affords the easiest implementation of all above discussed, requires very high processing times compared to the hardware solution, since it has an inappropriate architecture for real time applications.

Image size (pixels)	Census window size (pixels)	Time of processing FPGA	DSP	PC
192×144	3×3	$0.69ms$	$0.26s$	$33.29s$
192×144	5×5	$0.69ms$	$0.69s$	$34.87s$
192×144	7×7	$0.69ms$	$1.80s$	$36.31s$
384×288	3×3	$2.77ms$	$1.00s$	$145.91s$
384×288	5×5	$2.77ms$	$2.75s$	$151.39s$
384×288	7×7	$2.77ms$	$7.20s$	$158.20s$
640×480	3×3	$7.68ms$	$2.80s$	$403.47s$
640×480	5×5	$7.68ms$	$7.70s$	$423.63s$
640×480	7×7	$7.68ms$	$20.00s$	$439.06s$

Table 4. Performance comparison of different implementation.

We present a comparative analysis between our two architectures and four different FPGA implementations found in the literature. The first column of table 5 lays out the most common characteristics of the architectures. The second and third columns show the limitations, performance and consumed resources by our architectures using the RTL level design and the High level synthesis HLS (Ibarra-Manzano, Devy, Boizard, Lacroix & Fourniols, 2009), labeled as Design 1 and Design 2, respectively. The remaining columns show the corresponding values for the four architectures, labeled as Design 3 to 6. These architectures were designed by different authors. See their corresponding articles for more technical details (Naoulou et al., 2006), (Murphy et al., 2007), (Arias-Estrada & Xicotencatl, 2001) y (Miyajima & Maruyama, 2003) for Design 3 to 6. Besides all of these are FPGA implementations, they calculate dense disparity images from two stereo images. Our architecture could be directly compared with Design 3 and 4, since they use the Census transform algorithm for calculating the disparity map. We propose two essential improvements with respect to Design 3: the delay and the size of memory. These improvements directly affect the number of logic elements (area) that in our case increase. With respect to Design 2, we propose three important improvements: the delay, the area and the memory size. Again these improvements impact the performance, that is the processed image per second is lower. Although Design 4 has a good performance with respect to other designs, this is lower than our architecture performance. In addition, it uses a four-times-smaller image, it has a lower value of disparity measure and it consumes a bigger quantity of resources (area and memory). Our architecture cannot be directly compared with Designs 5 and 6, since they use the Sum Absolute of Differences (SAD) as a correlation measure. However, an interesting comparison point is the architecture performance required for calculating the disparity map, at the moment that an architecture uses only logic elements (Design 5) or when several accesses to external memories are used (Design 6). The big quantity of logic elements consumed by the architecture in Design 5 limits the size of the input images and the maximal disparity value. As a consequence, this architecture has a lower performance with respect to our architecture (Design 1). The Design 6 requires a large quantity of external memory that directly affects its performance with respect to our Design 1.

5. Implementation results

We are interested in obtaining the disparity maps relative to a image sequence acquired from a camera mounted in a moving vehicle or robot. It is important to point out the additional

	Design 1	Design 2	Design 3	Design 4	Design 5	Design 6
Measure	Census	Census	Census	Census	SAD	SAD
Image size	640×480	640×480	640×480	320×240	320×240	640×480
Window size	7×7	7×7	7×7	13×13	7×7	7×7
Disparity max	64	64	64	20	16	80
Performance	325	40	130	40	71	18.9
Latency (μs)	115	206	274	–	–	–
Area	12,188	6,977	11,100	26,265	4,210	7,096
Memory size	114 Kb	109 Kb	174 Kb	375 Kb	–	–

Table 5. Comparative table from different architectures.

constraint imposed by a vehicle in which the velocity is varying or very high. In this context, our architecture was tested for different navigational scenes using a stereo vision bank first mounted in a mobile robot and then in a vehicle. In this section, we present three operational environments. Figure 8 (a) and (b) respectively show the left and right images from the stereo vision bank. Dense disparity image depicts the disparity value in gray color levels in figure 8 (c). By examining this last image, we can determine that if the object is close to the stereo vision bank that means a big disparity value, so it corresponds to a light gray level. Otherwise, if the object is far from the stereo vision bank, the disparity value is low, which corresponds to a dark gray level. In this way, we observe that the gray color which represents the road in the resulting images gradually changes from light to dark gray level. We point out the right side of the image, where we can see the different tones of gray level corresponding to each vehicle in the parking. Since these vehicles are located at different depths from the stereo vision bank, the disparity map detects and assigns a corresponding gray color value.
The second test performed with the algorithm is shown in figure 9. In this case a white vehicle moves straightforward in our robot direction. This vehicle is detected in the disparity image and depicted with different gray color levels. Different depth points of the vehicle can be detected, since it is closer to our stereo vision bank than the vehicles parked at the right side of the scene. On the other hand, it is important to point out that sometimes the disparity validation fails because the similarity between left and right images is close. This problem is more significant when there are shadows close to the visual system (as in this experiment) producing several detection errors in the shadow zones.
In the last test (see figure 10), the stereo vision bank is mounted on a vehicle that is driven on a highway. This experimental test results in a difficult situation because the vehicle is driven at high-speed during the test. The left and right images (figure 10 (a) and (b) respectively) show a car that overtakes our vehicle. The figure 10 (c) shows the dense disparity map. We highlight all the different depths detected in the vehicle that overtakes our vehicle and how the gray color value in the highway becomes gradually darker until the black color which represents an infinity depth.

6. Back-projection for 3D environment reconstruction

Many applications use the obtained disparity image for the obstacles detection task because the association of disparity values with a certain depth in the real world is straightforward. However, maybe the most common application of the disparity image is the 3D reconstruction of the environment. The reconstruction method employs a technique called back-projection, which uses the intrinsic parameters of the camera and the disparity image for positioning one point in the real world.

(a) Left stereo image

(b) Right stereo image

(c) Result from FPGA implementation

Fig. 8. Stereo images acquired from a mobil robot during outdoor navigation: a) left image b) right image and c) the disparity map.

(a) Left stereo image

(b) Right stereo image

(c) Result from FPGA implementation

Fig. 9. Stereo images acquired from a mobile robot during outdoor navigation: a) left image b) right image and c) the disparity map.

Figures 11 (a) and (b) show the left image and the obtained disparity map respectively. Figure 11 (c) shows the reconstructed environment using the back-projection technique. Each point in the reconstructed scene was located with respect to a reference frame set in the stereo bank employing intrinsic/extrinsic parameters of the cameras and geometrical

(a) Left stereo image (b) Right stereo image (c) Result from FPGA implementation

Fig. 10. Stereo images acquired from a vehicle in the highway: a) left image b) right image and c) the disparity map.

(a) Left stereo image (b) Dense disparity image

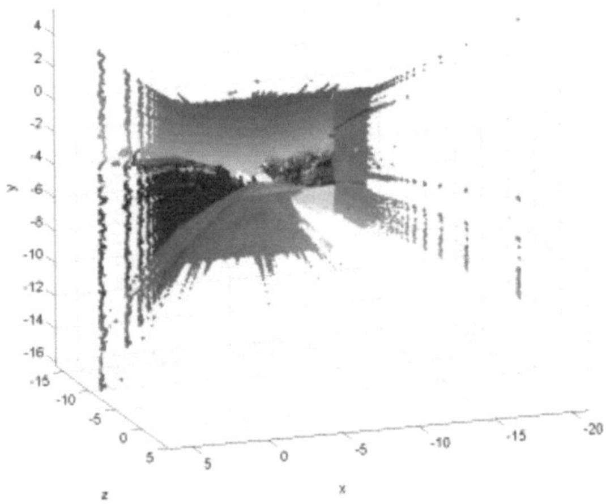

(c) 3D reconstruction

Fig. 11. 3D reconstruction from outdoor environment using dense disparity map obtained by our architecture.

assumptions. By examining figure 11 (c), we can see that most of the undefined disparity points were removed, thus the reconstruction is based on the well-defined depth-points. Finally, it is important to point out that the reconstruction of this environment results in a difficult task, since the robot with the stereo vision bank moves with a considerable velocity of 6 meters per second and in an outdoor environment. Therefore, the ideal conditions of controlled illumination and controlled vibrations do not hold, and this will be reflected in some images, making it more difficult to obtain the disparity map and, consequently, the scene reconstruction.

7. Conclusions and perspectives

The logic-programmable technology is known as an intermediary solution between the programmable processors and the dedicated VLSI circuits due mainly to its price, performance and power consumption. Furthermore, it is difficult to establish frontiers for delimiting logic-programmable technology applications because of their continual evolution. All of this makes this technology an attractive solution.

Nowadays, the FPGAs allow the development of hardware systems that overcome most of the limitations of real-time applications. However, the price and design time of the FPGA solutions make this technology a complicated tool in comparison with the software solutions. The designers must repeat the flow diagram of the design several times in order to overcome the performance limitations of the application, under the constraints imposed by always reducing the resources consumed by the circuit. At each iteration, the flow design could take several hours and in some cases days before converging into the optimal solution.

The high level synthesis allows us to reduce the design time of the algorithm with confidence that the resulting code will be equally efficient. This fact requires that the quality in the design be independent of the designer abilities. With the aim of efficiency, the high level synthesis must use design methods that take into account the specialization domain of the application.

We take advantage of rapidly-processing natural stereo images to use our architecture in real time applications. Resulting disparity images demonstrate the correct detection of different depth planes in stereo image pairs. However, resulting images present several fail detections that make images corrupt and noisy. In order to improve disparity image quality, we could include an additional measure of correlation to our current Hamming distance (such as Tanimoto distance) or the latter as the only correlation measure used. Both (Hamming and Tanimoto) resulted in disparity measures that could be linked in a unique disparity measure that will be more discriminative than our current one.

The improvements in the stereo vision architecture include an algorithm for auto-calibration, in order to reduce the error during disparity calculation. Also, with the auto-calibration process we eliminate the previous calibration problem. In this way, the stereo vision system will be more suitable with respect to the current version. In the case of the modules, we are working on their parametrization. This consists of developing auto-configurable modules in which we could directly vary the window sizes (both processing and search window), and this allows us to develop a reconfigurable system useful for different purposes.

8. Acknowledgments

This work was partially funded by the CONACyT with the project entitled "Diseño y optimización de una arquitectura para la clasificación de objetos en tiempo real por color y textura basada en FPGA"

9. References

Arias-Estrada, M. & Xicotencatl, J. M. (2001). Multiple stereo matching using an extended architecture, *in* G. Brebner & R. Woods (eds), *FPL '01: Proceeding of the 11th International Conference on Field-Programmable Logic and Applications*, Springer-Verlag, London, UK, pp. 203–212.

Coussy, P. & Morawiec, A. (2008). *High-Level Synthesis: from Algorithm to Digital Circuit*, 1 edn, Springer.

Dhanasekaran, D. & Bagan, K. B. (2009). High speed pipelined architecture for adaptive median filter, *European Journal of Scientific Research* 29(4): 454–460.

Ibarra-Manzano, M. (2011). *Vision multi-caméra pour la détection d'obstacles sur un robot de service: des algoritmes à un système intégré*, PhD thesis, Institut National des Sciences Appliquées de Toulouse, Toulouse, France.

Ibarra-Manzano, M., Almanza-Ojeda, D.-L., Devy, M., Boizard, J.-L. & Fourniols, J.-Y. (2009). Stereo vision algorithm implementation in fpga using census transform for effective resource optimization, *Digital System Design, Architectures, Methods and Tools, 2009. 12th Euromicro Conference on*, pp. 799 –805.

Ibarra-Manzano, M., Devy, M., Boizard, J.-L., Lacroix, P. & Fourniols, J.-Y. (2009). An efficient reconfigurable architecture to implement dense stereo vision algorithm using high-level synthesis, *2009 International Conference on Field Programmable Logic and Applications*, Prague, Czech Republic, pp. 444–447.

Masrani, D. & MacLean, W. (2006). A Real-Time large disparity range Stereo-System using FPGAs, *Computer Vision Systems, 2006 ICVS '06. IEEE International Conference on*, p. 13.

Miyajima, Y. & Maruyama, T. (2003). A real-time stereo vision system with fpga, *in* G. Brebner & R. Woods (eds), *FPL '03: Proceeding of the 13th International Conference on Field-Programmable Logic and Applications*, Springer-Verlag, London, UK, pp. 448–457.

Murphy, C., Lindquist, D., Rynning, A. M., Cecil, T., Leavitt, S. & Chang, M. L. (2007). Low-cost stereo vision on an fpga, *FCCM '07: Proceeding of the 15th Annual IEEE Symposium on Field-Programmable Custom Computing Machines*, IEEE Computer Society, Washington, DC, USA, pp. 333–334.

Naoulou, A., Boizard, J.-L., Fourniols, J. Y. & Devy, M. (2006). A 3d real-time vision sytem based on passive stereovision algorithms: Application to laparoscopic surgical manipulations, *Proceedings of the 2nd Information and Communication Technologies, 2006 (ICTTA)*, Vol. 1, IEEE, pp. 1068–1073.

Schmit, H. H., Cadambi, S., Moe, M. & Goldstein, S. C. (2000). Pipeline reconfigurable fpgas, *Journal of VLSI Signal Processing Systems* 24(2-3): 129–146.

Vega-Rodriguez, M. A., Sanchez-Perez, J. M. & Gomez-Pulido, J. A. (2002). An fpga-baed implementation for median filter meeting the real-time requirements of automated visual inspection systems, *Proceedings of th 10th Mediterranean Conference on Control and Automation*, Lisbon, Portugal, pp. 1–7.

Woodfill, J., Gordon, G., Jurasek, D., Brown, T. & Buck, R. (2006). The tyzx DeepSea g2 vision system, ATaskable, embedded stereo camera, *Computer Vision and Pattern Recognition Workshop, 2006. CVPRW '06. Conference on*, p. 126.

Zabih, R. & Woodfill, J. (1994). Non-parametric local transforms for computing visual correspondence, *ECCV '94: Proceedings of the Third European Conference on Computer Vision*, Vol. II, Springer-Verlag New York, Inc., Secaucus, NJ, USA, pp. 151–158.

6

Reality and Perception in Stereo Vision - Technological Applications

Humberto Rosas
Colombian Society of Geology
Colombian Institute of Geology and Minimg, Bogotá
Colombia

1. Introduction

In stereo vision, eyes capture two different views of a three-dimensional object. Retinal images are fused in the brain in a way that their disparities (or parallaxes) are transformed into depth perception, yielding a three-dimensional representation of the object in the observer's mind. The process of transforming parallax into depth perception is not entirely understood. The main question refers to the quantitative connection between these two variables, which creates a significant difference between real object and perceived image, that is, between reality and perception. In general, the theme of depth perception has been approached from different points of view.

In the first place, there is what could be called the geometric approach, because its methodology deals with relationships used in geometric optics for generating images. On this basis, several formulations were proposed for determining the vertical exaggeration perceived when aerial photographs are viewed stereoscopically (Aschenbrenner, 1952; Collins, 1981; Stone, 1951; Goodale, 1953; La Prade, 1972; 1973; 1978; Miller, 1960; Raasveldt, 1956; Yacoumelos, 1972; Yacoumelos,1973). At the end, none of these formulations has shown to be sufficiently reliable.

Another approach to depth perception in stereo vision is the psychological one. Differently from the geometric approach, observations are performed under conditions of natural vision (Norman et al, 1996; Rucker, 1977, Wagner, 1985). This methodology has the value of permitting the observer to make direct estimations of depth perception. In this manner, there is no risk of confusing perceptual lengths with real lengths. However, psychological observations on depth perception, rather than being quantitative, remain at a qualitative level.

A third approach to the study of depth perception is the physiological one. From that point, the attention centers on how the brain measures disparity form two retinal images. Qian, 1997 emphasizes the need of a better understanding of the brain function, and that any computational model must be based on real physiological data. On their turn, Backus, 2000; Backus, et al., 2001; and Chandrasekaran, et al., 2007 recognize that neural encoding of depth continues to be a mysterious subject. However, Mars, 1982, supports the belief that physiological details are not important for understanding visual perception, under certain mathematical assumptions. Consequently, he believes that physiological details do not become necessary for understanding the visual perception process.

Within the above framework of investigation, Rosas et al, 2010, have proposed a different approach to the stereo vision phenomenon. It could be called psychophysical approach because it establishes a mathematical connection between physical object and mental image, as a response to some conceptual inconsistencies showed by Rosas, 1986.
The present chapter will make special reference to mathematical relationships derived from the psychophysical approach, by taking into consideration that they may lead to innovations in the design of stereo viewing instruments. These possibilities for technological developments are described in the last part of this chapter.

2. Monocular vision

According to geometric optics, plane images are captured in the retinas and transmitted to the brain where they are projected outside to generate a mental representation of the object in space, or perceptual image. In monocular vision, the retinal image provides the brain with an exact representation of the object shape in two dimensions. As to object distance, the brain lacks geometric information enough to obtain telemetric data. Despite that, different types of pictorial cues, such as perspective, lights and shades, and logic judgments about size of familiar objects, allow the brain to make inferences concerning distance. In the absence of those cues, it becomes impossible for the brain to choose a specific location of object in space, as shown in Fig.1

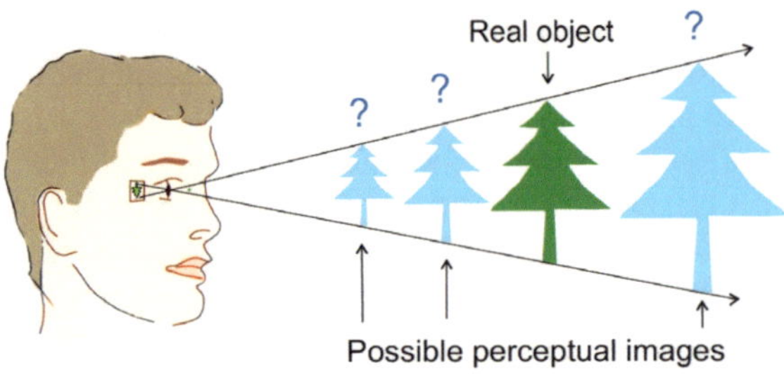

Fig. 1. Perception of a plane object in monocular vision. Geometric data does not provide information enough to define the object's location in space. Occasionally, some spatial cues might permit the observer to make reasonable inferences on distance.

3. Binocular vision

In binocular vision, a three dimensional image is obtained from two plane retinal images. In this case, depth perception is caused by the disparity (or parallax) created between the two retinal images. Experience shows that the perceived image normally does not fit the object shape but it appears deformed in depth, as illustrated in Fig. 2. The belief that we "see" the real word has led to erroneous conclusions, particularly derived from thinking that our mental perceptions are generated by intersection of optic rays. Though this methodology is valid for the real space, it shows inconsistencies regarding the perceptual space.
Regarding the perceptual space, there is a complex debate about whether it is Euclidean or not. Wagner 1985, Norman et al, 1996, propose the theory of a non-Euclidean space. They distinguish between the intrinsic structure of the perceptual space, which is Euclidean, and its extrinsic structure associated with the relationship between physical and perceived

space, which is non Euclidean. Rucker, 1977, suggests that the perceived space may be elliptic or positively curved.

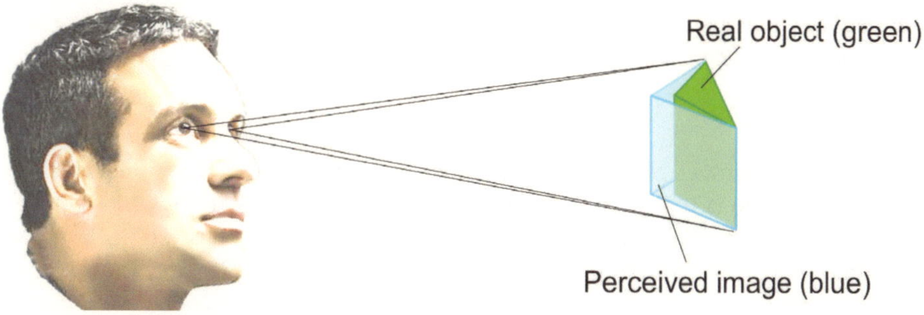

Fig. 2. Perception of an object in binocular vision. The three-dimensional object (green) appears deformed in depth in the perceived image (blue).

Indeed, it is not easy to obtain sound conclusions on perceptual space before establishing its precise relationship with the real space. The Cartesian formulation of Rosas et al, 2010 leads to conclude that the perceptual space is Euclidian. Something that eventually might result confusing refers to the scales of the perceptual space. In fact, its planar dimensions are linear, while its depth dimension is logarithmic.

4. Psychophysical nature of depth perception

A recent attempt to interrelate real space to perceptual space was made by Rosas et al , 2010. They developed an equation that connects real variables with perceptual ones. The whole analysis rests on the premise that parallax is the only information on depth available for the brain to build a three-dimensional model from two plane retinal images, so that parallax becomes the measure of depth perception. Other monocular and binocular cues supposed to influence depth perception, such as ordinal configural cues, perspective, occlusion, blur, vergence and accommodation (Burge et al., 2005, Landy et al., 1995; Mon-Williams et al; 2000; Allison et al., 2003), were not taken into consideration for the mathematical analysis.

In the formulations, an apostrophe placed after the symbols representing perceptual variables distinguishes them from the real ones. Experience shows that a perceptual depth interval $\Delta D'$ increases in accordance with its corresponding parallax ΔP. All of that leads to think of a direct proportionality existing between $\Delta D'$ and ΔP. That is,

$$\Delta D' = K \, \Delta P$$

Where K is a constant of proportionality. The above equation automatically connects a perceptual magnitude *($\Delta D'$)* with a real one *(ΔP)*. Through infinitesimal analysis, Rosas et al, 2010, arrived to the following equation:

$$D' = Kb \log D$$

Where D' is perceptual viewing distance, K is a constant characteristic of stereoscopic vision, b is eye base, or inter-pupillary distance, and D is real viewing distance.

The procedure of finding the numerical value of K may look operationally easy. However, the problem is that perceptual magnitudes, such as D', are not measurable physically as it is done in the real space. In order to overcome this difficulty, stereo drawings of pyramids were constructed and compared geometrically among them, in order to make reasonable estimations of depth perception. By applying this method, the value of *K*, for lengths given in centimeters, resulted to be 4.2. This value allows perceptual magnitudes to be solved in terms of real values. Then, the final equation is:

$$D' = 4.2b \log D \tag{1}$$

In psychophysical terms, *D′* can be considered a visual sensation caused by the visual stimulus of *D*. Then, it is curious though not surprising that the above equation happens to coincide with the psychophysical law proposed by Fechner, G.T., 1889, which states that sensation response increases proportionally to the logarithm of the stimulus intensity. That is:

$$R = k \log I \tag{2}$$

Where *R* is sensation response, *I* is stimulus intensity, and *k* is a constant characteristic of each sensorial mode, such as intensity of light, sound, smell, and weight sensation. The analogy between Eq. (1) and Eq. (2) would confirm the extension of the Fechner' Law to the stereo vision sensorial mode, and would indicate the psychophysical nature of depth perception. In Eq. (01), value 4.2 becomes the psychophysical constant for stereo vision (K).

5. Depth exaggeration

This expression is equivalent to "vertical exaggeration" widely used to designate the ratio of vertical scale to horizontal scale of the perceived object, when aerial photographs are viewed through a stereoscope. Evidently, under the optical specifications of common stereoscopes and according to the relationships used in the obtainment of aerial photographs, the terrain appears vertically exaggerated, a reason why the expression "vertical exaggeration" was adopted for referring to this increase in vertical scale. However, the increase of vertical scale is not a general rule. It is the reason why, for cases different from aerial photographs, the expression "depth exaggeration "is preferred in the present chapter.

Rosas et al. 2007a call the attention on the need of differentiating the vertical exaggeration of the three-dimensional model generated geometrically by intersection of optic rays (geometric exaggeration), from the vertical exaggeration of the image perceived in the observer's mind (perceptual exaggeration). The "vertical exaggeration" as it usually appears explained in books, normally refers to the geometric exaggeration (Gupta, 2003; Pandey, S., 1987). Its determination is a geometric procedure well known in photogrammetry. On the contrary, the perceptual exaggeration - central theme of this article - continues to be a controversial subject.

In fact, depth exaggeration measures the deformation an object shows in its third dimension when it is viewed stereoscopically, and therefore it will be a point of reference concerning stereo viewing instruments.

5.1. Depth exaggeration in natural stereo vision

Practically all of the mathematical formulations proposed for calculating depth exaggeration are derived from observations made under artificial stereo vision, by viewing aerial photographs with the aid of a stereoscope. The point is that this way has not led to significant conclusions regarding natural stereo vision.

Observations made under natural stereo vision have been focused from a psychological point of view. Regarding depth exaggeration, the psychological approach has arrived to the conclusion that the perceived space is increasingly compressed in depth at farther viewing distances (Norman et al, 1996, Wagner 1985,). In other terms, it means that depth exaggeration decreases with viewing distance. These observations are entirely valid, although they remain at a qualitative level, lacking of numerical results.

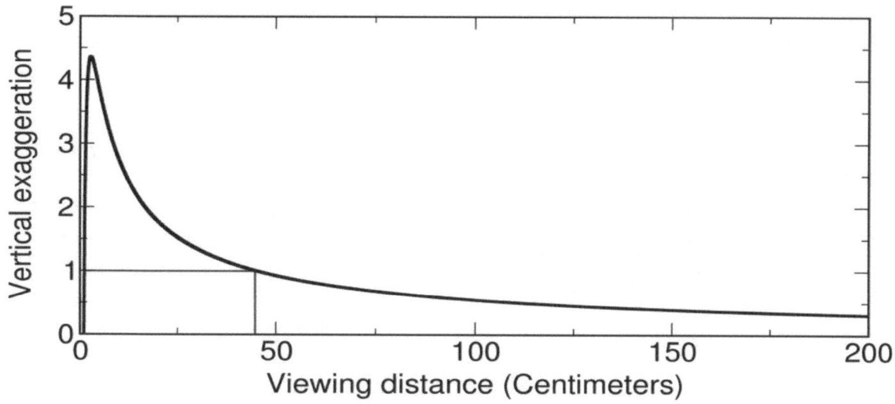

Fig. 3. Curve showing the variation of vertical exaggeration (or depth exaggeration) relative to viewing distance, in natural stereo vision, for an eye base of 6.5 cm. (Rosas et al, 2010).

A mathematical expression proposed by Rosas et al, 2010, provides elements for quantifying the phenomenon of depth exaggeration in natural stereo vision. The corresponding equation for depth exaggeration is:

$$E' = 4.2\frac{b}{D}\log D \quad (3)$$

Where E′ is depth exaggeration, 4.2 is the psychophysical constant K for stereo vision, *b* is eye base, and *D* is viewing distance. The graphic of this equation is showed in Fig. 3.
An exercise was done for determining the viewing distance from which a three- dimensional object is viewed with no deformation (*E′*=1) by a person having *b* = 6.5 cm. (a reasonable average for humans). Replacing values in Eq. (3), the following expression is obtained.

$$1 = 4.2\frac{6.5}{D}\log D \quad (4)$$

Hence, $D = 45cm.$
Then, 45 cm is the distance at which a three-dimensional object is viewed in its right shape. Rosas et al, 2010 called this distance "Realistic viewing distance". It is remarkable that 45 cm. becomes the distance at which humans handle most of their manual tools.
The graphic of Fig. 3 shows that vertical (or depth) exaggeration decreases with viewing distance, except for extremely short distances where the convergence of eye axes is abnormal. In the same figure the correlation of the value *E′*=1 with its correspondent *D*=45cm. is graphically indicated.

It is important to make clear that depth exaggeration is a punctual feature for a specific distance, upon the basis of infinitesimal depth intervals. In the graphic of Fig.3, E' decreases rapidly with viewing distance (D), up to the point that, for a distance of 100mt, $E'= 0.00546$, a value which may look apparently negligible; and even more if distances of kilometers are considered. However, this does not mean that depth perception becomes imperceptible, since at long viewing distances the observer is able to perceive great differences in depth. Though small depth intervals may be imperceptible, big depth intervals become quite significant within the whole field of vision.

In qualitative terms, the curve of Fig.3 coincides with the psychological observations made by Norman et al, 1996 and Wagner 1985, in the sense that perceptual space is progressively compressed as viewing distance increases.

5.2. Depth exaggeration in artificial stereo vision

Artificial stereo vision takes place when the observer does not see a three-dimensional object directly but through a pair of plane images. An example is the observation of aerial photographs with a stereoscope. In this case, the equation of depth exaggeration (E') takes the following form:

$$E' = 4.2\frac{B}{H}\log D \tag{5}$$

Where 4.2 is the psychophysical constant K for stereo vision, B is camera baseline, H is camera distance (or height of flight in the case of aerial photographs), and D is viewing distance. In the use of lenses, the viewing distance corresponds to the focal length of the ocular lenses. Then, another form of Eq. (5) is:

$$E' = 4.2\frac{B}{H}\log f \tag{6}$$

The ratio B/H can also be expressed in function of the convergence angle of camera axes (α), according to the following equation:

$$\frac{B}{H} = 2\tan\frac{\alpha}{2} \tag{7}$$

$$\text{Hence, } E' = 4.2 \times 2\tan\frac{\alpha}{2}\log f$$

In defining the characteristics of some stereoscopic instruments, such as microscopes, the use of α is preferred.

Before going into details concerning technological applications, it is worthwhile to point out the ubiquitous character of the psychophysical constant (K) that, for lengths given in centimeters, becomes equal to 4.2.

6. Technological applications

Technological applications refer to the design of instruments for obtaining a given degree of depth exaggeration, so that an object can be perceived as elongated or flattened as desired, or even with no deformation. Examples of these instruments are microscopes, telescopes, photo interpretation devices, simulators and, in general, stereoscopic media where perception is critical. Furthermore, taking into account that depth exaggeration varies with viewing distance according to a logarithmic function (Fig. 3), stereoscopic instruments can be designed to recreate artificially the perception of an object or scenery as viewed at a given distance in natural vision. In viewing instruments based on depth perception, its degree of precision is limited by the sensibility of the vision system.

In contrast to the above-mentioned instruments, there are the photogrammetric instruments that work upon the basis of measurements performed directly on real objects, virtually with any desired degree of precision. These instruments do not include depth perception data in their calculations, and therefore they are not a subject of the present chapter.

6.1 Interpretation of aerial photographs

In the observation of aerial photographs though a stereoscope, three stereo models come into play. One of them is the real model represented by the terrain being photographed. A second one is the geometric model, yielded by the intersection of optic rays according to both the geometry of rays under which photographs were taken, and to the geometry under which they are viewed. A third stereo model is the one perceived by the observer, or perceptual model (Fig.4.).

A normal experience in the interpretation of aerial photographs is that the real model is perceived vertically exaggerated. That is why the term "vertical exaggeration" was coined for referring to such a deformation in depth. However, this effect that is practically a rule in viewing aerial photographs, is not applicable to other cases of stereoscopy. For example, in natural vision the rule is just the opposite one: the model, rather than being vertically exaggerated, uses to appear flattened.

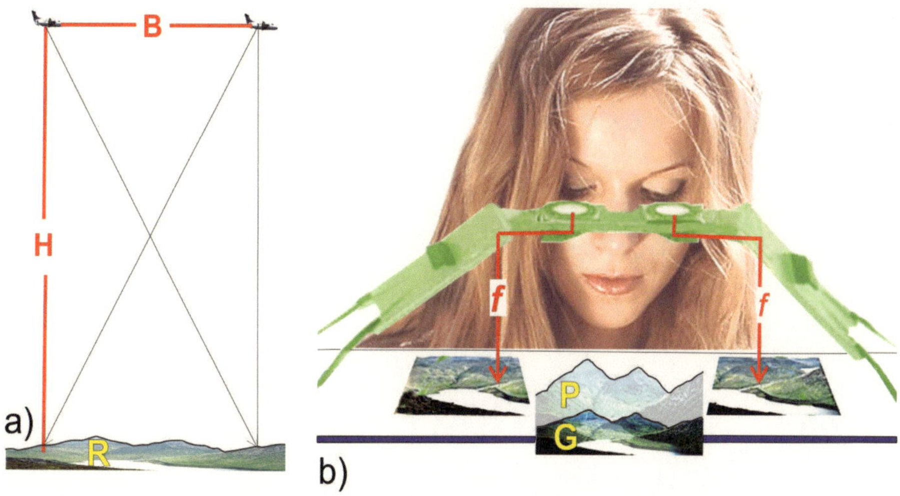

Fig.4. Interpretation of aerial photographs with the aid of a mirror stereoscope. a) Taking overlapping photographs from two camera positions. b) Viewing aerial photographs under a stereoscope. In the whole process, three stereo models come into play: real model (R) being photographed, geometric model (G) yielded by intersection of optical rays, and perceptual model (P) represented in the mind of the observer. Variables H, B, and f, influencing E, are indicated in red.

The vertical exaggeration of the perceptual model relative to the real one is given by Eq. 6 , that is:

$$E' = 4.2\frac{B}{H}\log f$$

Where B is camera base, H is camera distance (or height of flight), and f is focal length of the objective lenses. Note that the eye base of the observer does not influence E'.
The technological implication of this equation is that it connects a perceptual variable (E') with H, B and f representing instrument variables. Therefore, it permits real values to be converted into perceptual ones and vice versa. For example, in photo interpretation, the interpreter can make a rapid calculation of real topographic magnitudes such as dips and slopes in function of values perceived on the relief. The procedure consists in dividing perceived values by E'.

6.2 Microscopes and telescopes

Both microscopes and telescopes function under a similar optical principle, involving two main phases: 1) Capture of images through the objective lenses, and 2) observation of them through the oculars. The following equation, resulting from combining Eqs. (6) and (7), permits the degree of depth exaggeration to be calculated in function of objective and ocular features.

$$E' = 2\tan\frac{\alpha}{2} \times 4.2\log f \quad (8)$$

Where E' is depth exaggeration of the instrument, α is convergence angle of the objective lenses, and f is focal length of the ocular lenses. As it can be seen, E' depends on the convergence of objective lenses (α), and on the oculars' focal distance (f). The objectives' focal length influences the magnification factor of the instrument but it does not affect E'. Fig.5 shows a microscope where independent variables α and f are indicated in red.

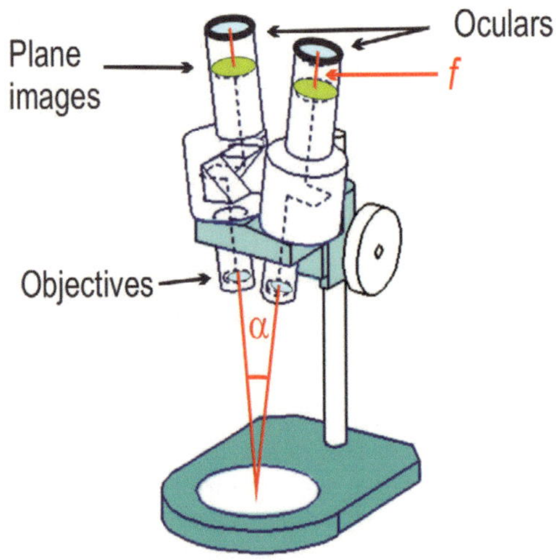

Fig. 5. Stereo microscope. Variables influencing vertical exaggeration are shown in red.

The technological conclusion is that Eq. (8) allows microscopes (and telescopes) variables to be conveniently interrelated for the observer to perceive an object with any desired depth exaggeration, between flattened and elongated, including with no deformation when E′ =1.

6.3 Stereo simulators

As explained before, in natural binocular vision, vertical exaggeration decreases with viewing distance, according to a logarithmic function. The mathematical relationships permits a scene perceived in natural vision to be recreated artificially by means of stereo images conveniently obtained and viewed.

Stereo viewing instruments for recreating reality might be applicable when objects are viewed through photographic images taken at a distance, for example by a robot, and required to be perceived as if the observer was located actually at a desired viewing distance. Another application is the production of videos that recreate the perception of a large area of land as viewed from an aircraft, in order to be implemented in flight simulators.

In addition, Eq. (3) for natural vision shows that the distance at which objects are viewed with no deformation in depth, is around 45 cm, referred to as "realistic viewing distance". It is significant that this viewing distance becomes the one used by humans in handling most of their familiar tools. On this basis, simulators could allow the operator to perceive objects as located at the optimal viewing distance for handling tools. An example of this application is the type of instruments used in telesurgery. Both stereo camera and stereo visor can be adjusted for the surgeon to perceive the area of intervention as if he was located at the realistic viewing distance, while the surgery tools are handled robotically.

6,3.1 Flight simulators

An example of instruments utilized for recreating artificially a scene as viewed in natural vision are flight simulators. In fact, they could also be applied for simulating the operation of different types of vehicles and crafts.

In the case of an aircraft, a landing maneuver can be simulated by a three-dimensional video that recreates the perception of the terrain as it is viewed in natural vision. The procedure comprises two stages: 1) stereoscopic recording of video images, and 2) viewing video images in a stereoscopic visor. In a landing maneuver there will be a prevailing viewing distance D where the pilot concentrates his attention - for instance 500 meters - that has to be established according to experience, type of aircraft, and other particular circumstances. Points located at the established viewing distance will be focused in the center of the visual field that, in this case, becomes considerably large.

The depth exaggeration (E'_N) perceived in natural stereovision, derived form Eq. (3), is:

$$E'_N = 4.2\frac{b}{D}\log D \tag{9}$$

Where b is the observer's eye base and D is the established viewing distance. On the other hand, the depth exaggeration (E'_I) perceived instrumentally in the visor is given by Eq. (6)

$$E'_V = 4.2\frac{B}{D}\log f \tag{10}$$

Where B is camera base and f is focal length of ocular lenses. The established viewing distance and the camera distance become the same , represented by D in both Eq. (9) and Eq. (10).

For matching natural vision with artificial vision, the key point consists in equalizing the depth exaggeration perceived in natural conditions, with the depth exaggeration perceived artificially in the visor. Therefore,

$$E'_N = E'_I$$

$$\text{Hence, } b\log D = B\log f \tag{11}$$

Where b is eye base, f is focal length of the ocular lenses and D is camera distance. Variable f is valid when lenses are used in the visor. If a three-dimensional screen is used, f corresponds to the observer-screen distance *(d)*. Hence

$$b\log D = B\log d \tag{12}$$

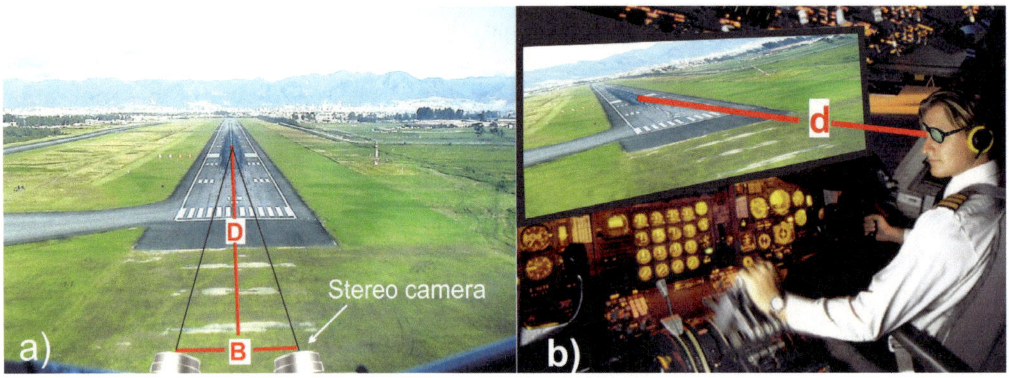

Fig. 6. Idealized flight simulator during a landing maneuver. a) Registering images in a stereo camera. b) Viewing stereo images in a three-dimensional screen. Variables *B, D* and *d*, influencing *E'*, are indicated in red.

The technological conclusion is that, for producing a video that allows the observer to reproduce artificially the perception of a scene as if he was located actually at a given distance, it is necessary that b ,D, B and f (or d), satisfy Eq. (11) or (12).

6.3.2 Robotic tools

They are instruments designed for manipulating tools by means of robotic hands that are controlled by visual perception. Examples of them are those used in telesurgery. In this instance, the surgeon sees the surgical tools through a pair of video images (Fig.7).

According to Eq. (6), when an object is viewed through stereo images, the depth exaggeration *(E')* takes the following expression

$$E' = 4.2\frac{B}{H}\log f$$

or in function of α according to Eq. (7)

$$E' = 4.2 \times 2 \tan\frac{\alpha}{2} \log f$$

Where α is convergence of camera axes, and f is focal length of the ocular lenses. For a surgeon to perceive the field of intervention in optimal conditions, as viewed under natural vision, it is necessary that E' equals one. Then,

$$1 = 4.2 \times 2 \tan\frac{\alpha}{2} \log f \quad (13)$$

The technological conclusion regarding telesurgery is that viewing instruments can be arranged to make the surgeon perceive his operating field with no deformation, as viewed in natural vision at a distance of about 45 cm. To reach that purpose it is necessary that variables ***α*** (or its equivalent in terms of *B* and *H*) and *f*, satisfy Eq. 13.

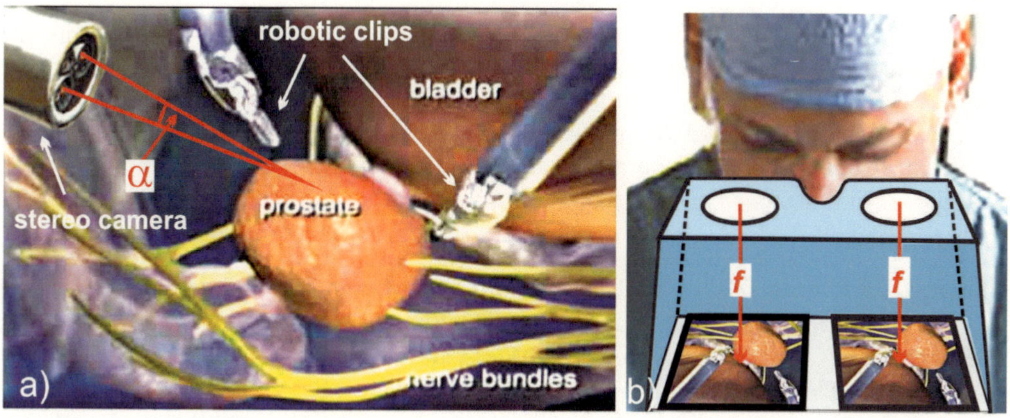

Fig, 7. Two phases of the vision process used in telesurgery. a) Video images recorded by a stereo camera when the surgeon performs a laparoscopic prostatectomy. b) The surgeon observes the stereo images through a visor that allows him to perceive the three-dimensional effect. Variables *α* and *f* influencing depth exaggeration are indicated in red. http://i.ytimg.com/vi/ChO9CUwr_2Y/0.jpg

7. Conclusion

In stereo vision, retinal disparities are mentally converted into depth perception, in a way that the real depth magnitudes are not always reproduced accurately in the perceived image. As a result, reality is perceived deformed in depth. Experiments have shown the metric correlation between real and perceptual depth to follow a logarithmic function that happened to coincide with the Psychophysical Law of Fechner, 1889, connecting stimulus with sensation. Indeed, stimulus is associated with reality while sensation is related to perception.

The above considerations have implications concerning the geometric nature of the perceptual space. The Cartesian connection between reality and perception leads to conclude that the perceptual space is Euclidean, its third dimension being logarithmic, while its plane dimensions remain linear.

The fact that real lengths can be expressed mathematically in terms of perceptual lengths opens possibilities for technological developments, particularly in the design of stereo viewing instruments such as stereoscopes, microscopes, telescopes and stereoscopic viewers.

It is important to emphasize that the technological applications mentioned above refer to instruments in which perception is critical. This is not the case of photogrammetric instruments dealing with the external reality, where three-dimensional perception becomes only an aid for recognizing objects in space, rather than for measuring them. In general, we can say that photogrammetric instruments (analog and digital) use fundamentally linear functions, whereas perception instruments work upon the basis of logarithmic functions.

8. Acknowledgements

The author expresses his gratitude to Drs. Henry Villegas and Orlando Navas, from the Colombian Institute of Geology and Mining (INGEOMINAS) Bogotá, Colombia, for their scientific and logistic support, including the final revision of the manuscript. The Colombian Society of Geology assumed the publishing costs. The mathematical formulations were verified instrumentally in the laboratories of INGEOMINAS.

9. References

Allison, R.S., Rogers, B.J., & Bradshaw, M.F. (2003). Geometric and Induced Effects in Binocular Stereopsis and Motion Parallax. *Vision Research*, Vol. 43, pp.1879-1893.

Aschenbrenner, C.M., (1952). A Review of Facts and Terms Concerning the Stereoscopic Effect. *Photogrammetric Engineering*, Vol. 18, No. 5, pp.818-825.

Backus, B.T., (2000). Stereoscopic vision: What's the First Step?. *Current Biology*, Vol.10, pp. R701-R703.

Backus, B.T., Fleet, D.J., Parker, A.J., & Heeger, D.J. (2001). Humancortical Activity Correlates with Stereoscopic Depth Perception. *Journal of Neurophysiology*, Vol.86, pp.2054-2068.

Burge, J., Peterson, M.A., & Palmer, S.E. (2005). Ordinal Configural Cues Combine with Metric Disparity in Depth Perception. *Journal of Vision*, Vol.5, pp.534-542.

Chandrasekaran, C., V. Canon, Dahmen, J.C., Kourtzi, Z. & Welchman, A.E. (2007). Neural Correlates of Disparity Defined Shape Discrimination in the Human Brain. *Journal of Neurophysiology*, Vol. 97, pp.1553-1565.

Collins, S.H., (1981). Stereoscopic Depth Perception. *Photogrammetric Engineering*, Vol. 47, No.1, pp. 45-52.

Fechner, G.T., (1889). *Elemente der psychophysik, Vol. 1,* Breitkopf and Härte,Leipzig, Germany, Translated into English by H E Adler, 1966. *Elements of Psychophysics Vol. 1,* New York: Holt,Rinehart, and Winston.

Goodale, E.R., (1953). An Equation for Approximating the Vertical Exaggeration of a Stereoscopic View. *Photogrammetric Engineering,* Vol. 19. No. 4, pp. 607–616.

Gupta, R.P., (2003). *Remote Sensing Geology*, Springer, 680 p.

La Prade, G.L., (1978). Stereoscopy. *Manual of Photogrammetry,* American Society of Photogrammetry, Fourth edition, Chapter 10, pp. 519–534.

La Prade, G.L., (1973). Stereoscopy - Will Data or Dogma Prevail?. *Photogrammetric Engineering*, Vol, 39, No. 12, pp. 1271–1275.

La Prade, G.L., (1972). Stereoscopy - A More General Theory. *Photogrammetric Engineering,* Vol.38, No.10, pp. 1177–1187.

Landy, M.S., Maloney, L.T., Johnston, E.B. & Young, M. (1995). Measurement and Modeling of Depth Cue Combination: In Defense of Weak Fusion. *Vision Research,* Vol.35, No.3, pp. 389–412.

Marr, D., 1982. *Vision: A Computational Investigation into the Human Representation and Processing of Visual Information,* W. H. Freeman and Company, New York, 397 p.

Miller, C.L., 1958. Vertical Exaggeration in the Stereo Space-image and its Use, *Photogrammetric Engineering* 26(5):815–818.

Mon-Williams, M., J Tresilian, R. & Roberts, A. (2000). Vergence Provides Veridical Depth Perception from Horizontal Retinal Image Disparities. *Experimental Brain Research,* Vol. 133, pp. 407–413.

Norman, J.F., Farley, J., Todd, J.T., Perotti, V.J. & Tittle, J.S. (1996). The Visual Perception of Three- dimensional Length. *Journal of Experimental Psychology,* Vol. 22, No.l, pp. 173–186.

Pandey, S., 1987. *Principles and Applications of Photogeology,* New Age International, - Science - 366 pages

Qian, N., 1997. Binocular Disparity and the Perception of Depth, Review. *Neuron,* Vol.18, pp. 359–368.

Raasveldt, H.C. (1956). The Stereomodel, How it is Formed and Deformed. *Photogrammetric Engineering,* Vol 22, No.9, pp. 708–726.

Rosas, H., (1986). Vertical Exaggeration in Stereo-vision: Theories and Facts. *Photogrammetric Engineering & Remote Sensing,* Vol.52, No.11, pp. 1747–1751.

Rosas, H.; Vargas, W.; Cerón, A.; Domínguez, D. & Cárdenas, A. (2007). Psychophysical Approach to the Measurement of Depth Perception in Stereo Vision, *Virtual Reality,* HCII 2007, LNCS 4563, pp. 358–366, Springer-Verlag Berlin Heidelberg 2007

Rosas, H.; Vargas, W.; Cerón, A.; Domínguez, D. & Cárdenas, A. (2007). Toward the Solution of the Vertical Exaggeration Enigma in Stereo Vision, *Ciencia e Ingeniería Neogranadina,* Vol. 17, No. 2, pp. 83-93, ISSN 0124-8170, Bogotá, Colombia

Rosas, H.; Vargas, W.; Cerón, A.; Domínguez, D. & Cárdenas, A. (2010). A Mathematical Expression for Stereoscopic Depth Perception. *Photogrammetric Engineering & Remote Sensing,* Vol. 76, No. 3, pp. 301–306.

Rucker, R. V. B. (1977). *Geometry, relativity and the fourth dimension.* New York: Dover.

Singleton, R. (1956). Vertical Exaggeration and Perceptual Models, *Photogrammetric Engineering,* Vol.22, No.9, pp. 175–178.

Stone, K.H., (1951). Geographical Air-photo Interpretation. *Photogrammetric Engineering,* Vol.17, No. 5, pp. 754–759.

Wagner, M. (1985). The Metric of Visual Space. *Perception & Psychophysics,* Vol.38, pp. 483-495.

Yacoumelos, N.G.,1972. The Geometry of the Stereomodel. *Photogrammetric Engineering,* Vol.38, No.8, pp. 791–798.

7

Stereo Vision and its Application to Robotic Manipulation

Jun Takamatsu
Nara Institute of Science and Technology (NAIST)
Japan

1. Introduction

A robot is expected to provide a service to us in our daily-life environment. Thus, it is easy to find robots that can achieve a task, such as home cleaning performed by the iRobot *Roomba*[1] or entertainment provided by the Sony *Aibo*. Unlike the situation in a plant, the daily-life environment changes sequentially. Before performing a task, it is necessary to observe the environment. Since the motion and manipulation done by a robot occur in a 3D world, gathering 3D information and not 2D information is inevitable. For example, such information helps us achieve semi-automatic robot programming (Ikeuchi & Suehiro (1994); Kuniyoshi et al. (1994)).

There are many kinds of devices to obtain 3D information. They are roughly classified into two types: active sensors and passive sensors. What distinguishes these two types is the capacity of the sensor to output energy (*e.g.*, emit light) to the outer world. As an example of active sensors, a laser sensor measures the distance using the duration since the light is emitted until it captures the reflected light.

Among the passive sensors, stereo vision is the simplest device to obtain 3D information. A stereo vision system employs at least two separate imaging devices, as in the case of human vision. Generally, the active sensors are better in accuracy than the passive sensors[2]. Although this may mean that human stereo vision suffers from inaccuracy of the obtained 3D information, we unconsciously employ prior knowledge to compensate for this.

Les us consider estimation of a 6-DOF object trajectory, which is required in various kinds of robotic manipulation, such as pick-and-place and assembly. To reduce the inaccuracy in the estimation, some constraints about the trajectory are necessary. For example, if it is previously known that the trajectory is a straight line, we reduce the inaccuracy by minimally deforming the trajectory to align it to the line. We will introduce prior knowledge into an actual robot application.

In this chapter, we will first present an overview of the stereo vision system and a method for localization using 3D data (Section 2). We will describe a method for using the contact relation (Section 3) as prior knowledge; in real world, rigid objects do not penetrate each other. Also,

[1] http://www.irobot.com

[2] However, the progress of the computer vision technology and a better benchmark data set fill the gap between them. See http://vision.middlebury.edu/stereo/.

we will describe a method for using constraints by some mechanical joint (Section 4); the type of mechanical joint defines the type of trajectory. Besides, we will introduce 3D modeling using implicit polynomials, which is robust to noise in modeling of primitive shape (Section 5). Finally we will present a conclusion for this chapter (Section 6).

2. Reviews

2.1 Stereo vision

Generally, an image represents the 3D world by projecting it onto a 2D image plane. In this sense, 3D shape reconstruction from a single image is an ill-posed problem. To simply solve this problem, it is possible to use at least two images captured from different viewpoints, *i.e.*, stereo vision. If the simple pin-hole camera model is assumed and the location of an object on both images is known, the triangulation technique outputs the 3D position or depth of the object. Note that geometric properties of both cameras are calibrated (Tsai (1986); Zhang (2000)).

Usually, it is required to obtain depths in all pixels of one image. Which means that is necessary to estimate the correspondence among all pixels. Unfortunately, this task is quite difficult. Assuming that the photometric properties of the camera are already calibrated[3], the corresponding pixels tend to have the same pixel values. In other words, the difference between these values is regarded as the degree of correspondence. If the range of depth is assumed, the candidates of the correspondences are restricted by searching the minimum differences within the range.

It is difficult to estimate the correspondence only from the single pixel observation. There are two types of solution methods. The first method consists of estimating the correspondence from the observation of a small region around the pixel. The other method consists of using prior knowledge, such as depths on the image that are usually smooth except on occluding boundaries of objects. Although these two methods are efficient for resolving the ambiguity in the correspondence, it is necessary to pay attention to the handling of the occluding boundaries. Further, the first method suffers from poor estimation of the correspondences in the texture-less region.

In summary, the depth image is estimated by the following steps (Scharstein & Szeliski (2002)):

1. matching cost computation
2. cost (support) aggregation
3. disparity computation or optimization
4. disparity refinement

The first step corresponds to calculating the difference in pixel values and the second step corresponds to the first method for solving the ambiguity. The second method is included in Step 3. Generally, the use of the second method achieves better performance in stereo vision. Please see the details in Scharstein & Szeliski (2002).

[3] Roughly speaking, when two calibrated cameras capture the same Lambertian object under the same illumination, the pixel values of the two images are the same.

When estimating the correspondences by the second method, it is necessary to minimize the following energy function:

$$E = \min_{d} \sum_{i \in I} C_1(i, d(i)) + \sum_{i,j \in I, i \neq j} C_2(i, j, d(i), d(j)), \tag{1}$$

where the term $d(i)$ represents the depth in the pixel i, and the set I represents the image region. The term C_1 is determined by one pixel. On the other hand, the term C_2 is determined by the relationship of two pixels. It is possible to think about the relationship of more than two pixels (referred to as *higher order term*).

Graph cuts (Boykov & Kolmogorov (2004)) and belief propagation (Felzenszwalb & Huttenlocher (2006)) are very interesting methods for minimizing the function as shown in Eq. (1). Although both methods suffer from difficulties in handling the higher order terms, recently these difficulties have been circumvented (Ishikawa (2009); Lan et al. (2006); Potetz (2007)). Although the Graph cuts may achieve a better performance in the optimization, it is very useful to take advantage of parallel computing by a Graphic Processing Unit (GPU) in the belief propagation since it easily accelerates the calculation (Brunton et al. (2006)).

2.2 Localization

Although the methods described in Section 2.1 provide us with the 3D information of the world, it is further needed to localize the target objects in order to estimate the interaction of the objects, which is very important especially in robotics applications. We assume that the 3D model of the target object is previously given.

There are two kinds of localization: rough localization and fine localization. The rough localization includes object detection and estimates rough correspondence between the model and the observed 3D data. The result of the rough localization is usually used as the input of the fine localization. The fine localization obtains the location of the object by precisely aligning the model and the observed 3D data.

The rough localization can be classified into two types: one that uses local descriptors and the other one that uses global descriptors. The first method calculates a descriptor of a point to distinguish it from the other points based on its local shape. The descriptor should be invariant to rigid transformation. The correspondence is estimated by comparing two descriptors. The idea is very similar to the descriptors in 2D images, such as SIFT (Lowe (2004)) and SURF (Bay et al. (2008)). For example, geometric hashing (Wolfson & Rigoutsos (1997)) calculates the descriptors from the minimum number of neighborhood points to satisfy the invariant. Spin images (Johnson & Hebert (1999)) uses point distribution in polar coordinates as descriptors. Once the correspondences are given, the rigid transformation is calculated by Umeyama (1991). Also, RANSAC (Fischler & Bolles (1981)) is useful to detect the erroneous correspondences.

The latter methods calculate one descriptor in each object. From the definition, a change of the descriptor by the rigid transformation is easily calculated. The rough localization is estimated by matching two descriptors. Geometric moment (Flusser & Suk (1994)) aligns the two objects by matching principal axes. Extended Gaussian Image (EGI) (*e.g.*. Kang & Ikeuchi (1997)) uses the distribution of the surface normal directions as a descriptor. The use of the spherical harmonics accelerates the localization (Makadia et al. (2006)). Spherical Attribute

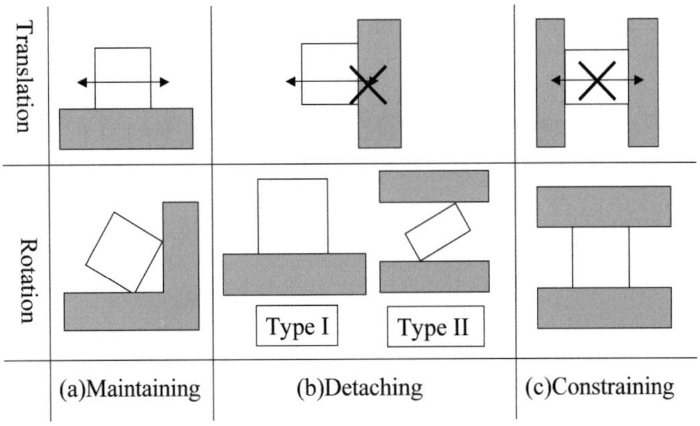

Fig. 1. Types of displacement. Considering the horizontal translation in the upper row, translation from left to right columns are unconstrained, partially constrained, and fully constrained. Considering the rotation in the lower row, rotation from left to right columns are unconstrained, partially constrained, and fully constrained as similar to the upper case. To reduce the vision errors while avoiding drastic changes in the original data, these three types should be distinguished.

Image (SAI) (Hebert et al. (1995)) represents the distribution of curvatures on the spherical coordinates.

In the fine localization, the key is how to estimate the correspondences in a fine resolution. The iterative closest point (Besl & McKay (1992); Chen & Medioni (1991)) is a pioneer work on the fine localization and regards the closest point as the correspondence. There are many variants with respect to the calculation of the correspondence and the evaluation function for the registration. Please see Rusinkiewicz & Levoy (2001). The output from the stereo vision system is relatively inaccurate, it is very important to make the fine localization robust to noise. To do so, a robust estimator, such as M-estimator (Huber (1981)), is normally used, such as Wheeler & Ikeuchi (1995).

3. Vision error correction using contact relations

Consider a moving object that comes into contact with another object or the environment. Due to the vision errors, in the imaginary world of the robot, the object possibly penetrates another object. The difference between the real world and the imaginary world makes more difficult to estimate the interaction of the objects. We introduce the use of contact information to reduce the vision errors. We assume that all the objects are polyhedral and concentrate on the two-object relationship; one object (referred to as *moving object*) moves and the other object (referrer to as *fixed object*) is fixed. Even by such simplification, the vision error correction is difficult due to the non-linearity (Hirukawa (1996)).

However, as shown in Fig. 1, local displacement along one direction (horizontal translation in the upper row and rotation in the lower row) is classified into three types: no constraint, partially constraint, and fully constraint. In order to reduce the vision errors while avoiding drastic changes in the original data, it would be better to keep the information corresponding to unconstrained direction.

We propose two types of methods for vision error correction using the contact relations. The contact relation represents a set of pairs of contacting elements (vertex, edge, and face). One method (Takamatsu et al. (2007)) relies on the non-linear optimization and often contaminates the unconstrained displacement. The other method (Takamatsu et al. (2002)) employs only the linear method. Although at least one solution which satisfies the contact relation is required, the optimality holds in this method.
The overview of the method is as follows:

1. Calculate the object configuration which satisfies the constraint on the contact relation using the non-linear optimization method (Takamatsu et al. (2007)). Note that we accept any configurations.
2. Formulate the equation of feasible infinitesimal displacement using the method (Hirukawa et al. (1994))
3. Calculate the optimum configuration by removing the redundant displacement that is derived from the non-linear optimization.

Hirukawa *et al.* proposed a method for introducing the constraint on the contact relation between two polynomial objects (Hirukawa et al. (1994)). They proved that the infinitesimal displacement that maintains the contact relation can be formulated as Eq. (2), where N is the number of pairs of contacting elements, $\mathbf{p}_i$ is the position of the i-th contact in the world coordinates, $\mathbf{f}_{ij}$ ($\in R^3$) is the normal vector of the separate plane[4], $M(i)$ is the number of separate planes of the i-th contact, and the 6D vector $[\mathbf{s}_0, \mathbf{s}_1]$ represents infinitesimal displacement in the screw representation (Ohwovoriole & Roth (1981)).

$$\bigcap_{i}^{N} \bigcap_{j}^{M(i)} \mathbf{f}_{ij} \cdot \mathbf{s}_1 + (\mathbf{p}_i \times \mathbf{f}_{ij}) \cdot \mathbf{s}_0 = 0. \tag{2}$$

In the screw representation, the vector $\mathbf{s}_0$ represents the rotation axis. Introducing the constraint only about the term $\mathbf{s}_0$ gives us the range of the feasible rotation axis as Eq. (3).

$$\bigcap_{i}^{n} \mathbf{g}_i \cdot \mathbf{s}_0 = 0. \tag{3}$$

The non-linearity is only derived from the non-linearity in the orientation. If the optimum orientation is already known, the issue on the vision error correction is simply solved using the least linear minimization. The method for calculating the optimum orientation varies according to the rank of Eq. (3), because the constraint is semantically varied. If the rank is three, the optimum orientation is uniquely determined. We only use the orientation obtained by the non-linear optimization. If the rank is zero, the original orientation is used.
Figure 2 shows the case where the rank is two. The upper left and the upper right images represent the orientation before and after the vision error correction by the non-linear optimization, respectively. The rotation about the axis shown in the lower right image is the redundant displacement, because this displacement does not change the contact relation. The optimum orientation is obtained by removing this displacement.

[4] For example, in the case where some vertex on the moving object make contact with some face on the fixed object, the vector $\mathbf{f}_{ij}$ is equal to the outer normal of the face.

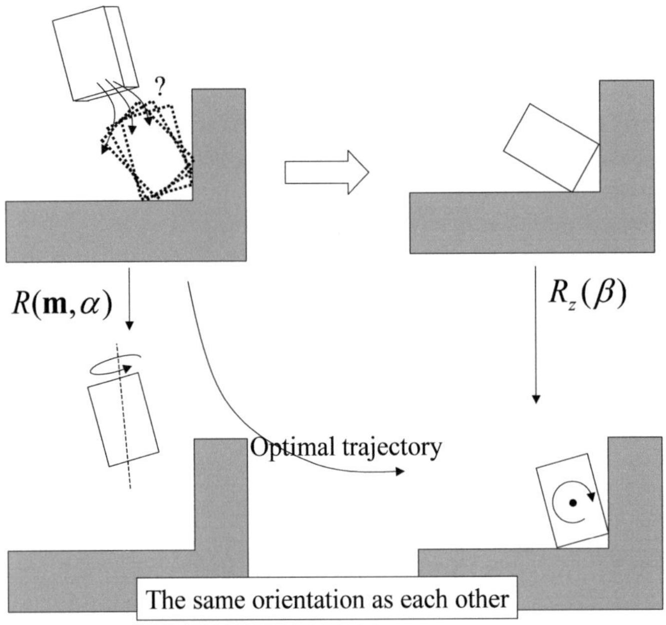

Fig. 2. Redundant orientation in the case where the rank is two. The upper left and the upper right images represent the orientation before and after the vision error correction by the non-linear optimization, respectively. The lower right image represents the optimum orientation; the rotation about the axis shown in the lower right image is the redundant displacement, because this displacement does not change the contact relation.

We define the local coordinates A, where the z-axis is defined as the axis of the redundant displacement, which is obtained from Eq. (3). Let ${}^{A}\Theta_E$ and ${}^{A}\Theta_S$ be the orientation before and after the vision-error correction in the local coordinates. The orientation ${}^{A}\Theta_E$ is translated to the orientation ${}^{A}\Theta_S$ by the following two steps:

1. rotation about the z-axis while maintaining the contact relation
2. rotation about the axis **m** which is on the xy-plane.

These two steps are formulated as Eq. (4), where $\mathbf{R}_*(\theta)$ ($\in$ SO(3)) is a θ [rad] rotation about $*$-axis, $\mathbf{R}(\mathbf{m}, \alpha)$ is a α [rad] rotation about the axis **m**.

$$\mathbf{R}(\mathbf{m}, \alpha)^{A}\Theta_S = \mathbf{R}_z(\beta)^{A}\Theta_E. \tag{4}$$

By solving this equation, the terms $\alpha, \beta, \mathbf{m}$ are calculated. The first rotation is the redundant displacement and the optimum orientation ${}^{A}\Theta_{opt}$ in the local coordinates is obtained by

$${}^{A}\Theta_{opt} = \mathbf{R}(\mathbf{m}, \alpha)^{A}\Theta_S. \tag{5}$$

Figure 3 shows the case where the rank is one. We define the local coordinates A, where the z-axis is the constrained DOF in rotation, which is obtained from Eq. (3). Let ${}^{A}\Theta_E$ and ${}^{A}\Theta_S$ be the orientation before and after the vision-error correction in the local coordinates. Similarly in the case where the rank is two, the orientation is translated to the orientation ${}^{A}\Theta_S$ by the following two steps:

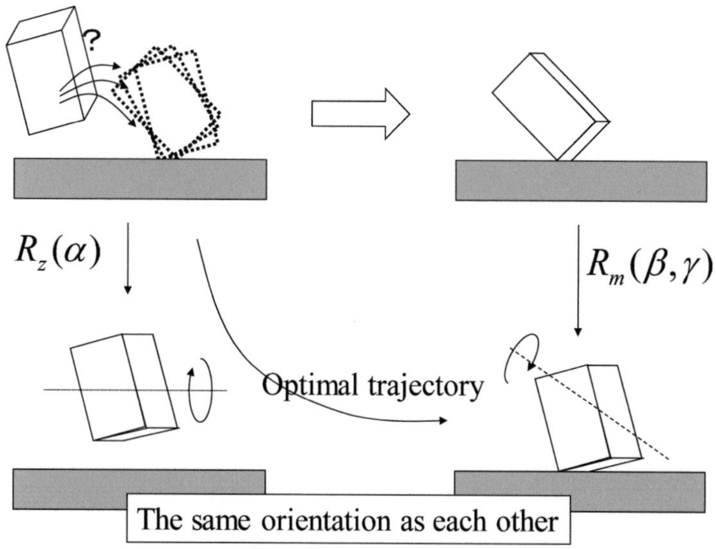

Fig. 3. Redundant displacement in the case where the rank is one. The upper left and the upper right images represent the orientation before and after the vision error correction by the non-linear optimization, respectively. The lower right image represents the optimum orientation; the rotation about the axis shown in the lower right image is the redundant displacement, because this displacement does not change the contact relation.

1. rotation while maintaining the contact relation
2. rotation about the z-axis

These two steps are formulated as Eq. (6),

$$\mathbf{R}_z(\alpha)^A\Theta_S = \mathbf{R}_m(\beta,\gamma)^A\Theta_E, \tag{6}$$

where $\mathbf{R}_m(\beta,\gamma)$ is the rotation to maintain the contact relation and has two DOF. The DOF of Eq. (6) is three and thus is solvable. The optimum orientation ${}^A\Theta_{opt}$ in the local coordinates is obtained by

$${}^A\Theta_{opt} = \mathbf{R}_z(\alpha)^A\Theta_S. \tag{7}$$

Unfortunately, the formulation of $\mathbf{R}_m(\beta,\gamma)$ varies case-by-case and there is no general rule. We assume that the rank becomes two, only when (1) some edge of the moving object makes contact with some face of the fixed object or when (2) some face of the moving object makes contact with some edge of the fixed object. These are common cases.
Consider the case 1 (see Fig. 4), a β [rad] rotation about the axis 1 followed by a γ [rad] rotation about the axis 2 maintains the contact relation. Thus the term $\mathbf{R}_m(\beta,\gamma)$ is formulated as:

$$\mathbf{R}_m(\beta,\gamma) = \mathbf{R}(\mathbf{n},\gamma)\mathbf{R}(\mathbf{l},\beta), \tag{8}$$

where $\mathbf{n}$ is the surface normal and $\mathbf{l}$ is the edge direction.
Consider the case 2 (see Fig. 5), a β [rad] rotation about the axis I followed by a γ [rad] rotation about the axis II maintains the contact relation. Thus the term $\mathbf{R}_m(\beta,\gamma)$ is formulated as:

$$\mathbf{R}_m(\beta,\gamma) = \mathbf{R}(\mathbf{l},\gamma)\mathbf{R}(\mathbf{n},\beta). \tag{9}$$

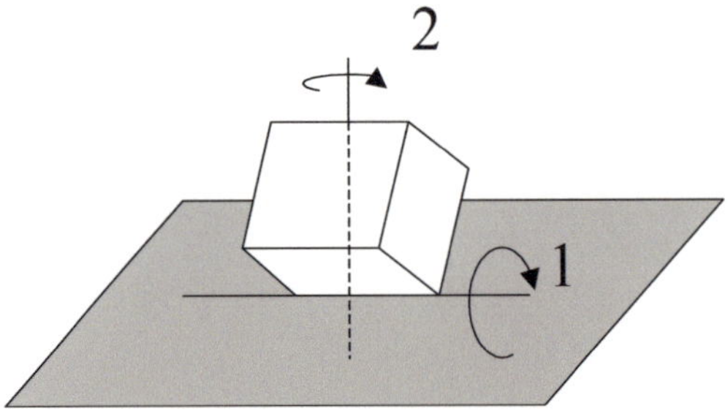

Fig. 4. Case 1: some edge of the moving object makes contact with some face of the fixed object

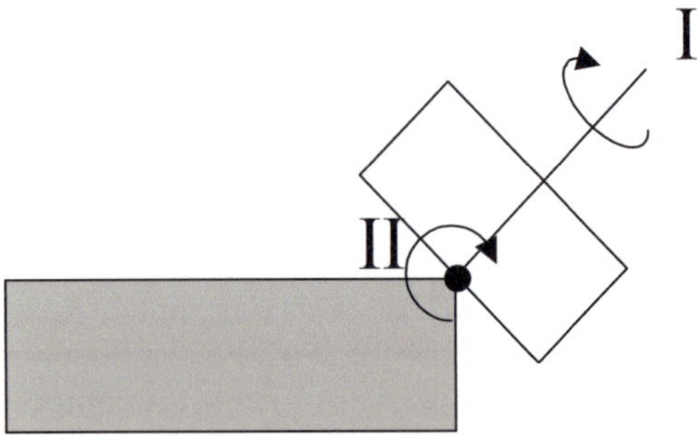

Fig. 5. Case 2: some face of the moving object makes contact with some edge of the fixed object

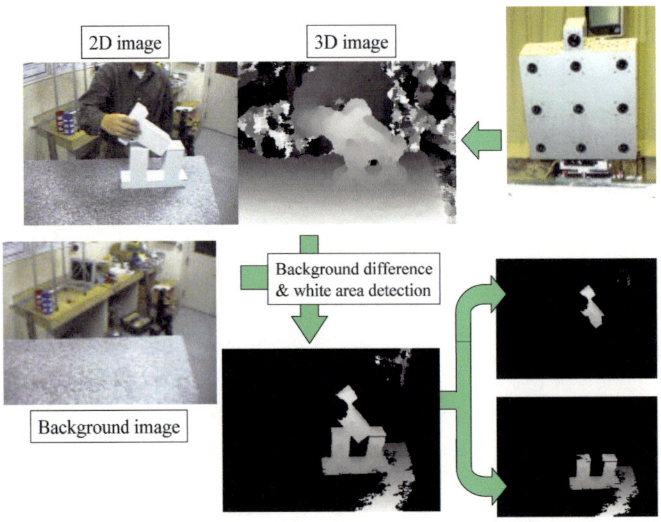

Fig. 6. Vision system and the overview of the vision algorithm

In both cases, Eq. (6) can be solved.

Result In experiments in this section, we use the vision system in Fig. 6. Since the depth image is obtained in real-time, this vision system uses only the first method to solve the

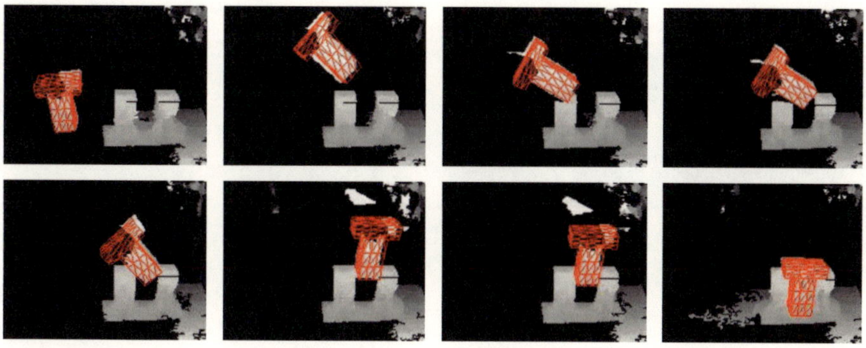

Fig. 7. Tracking result

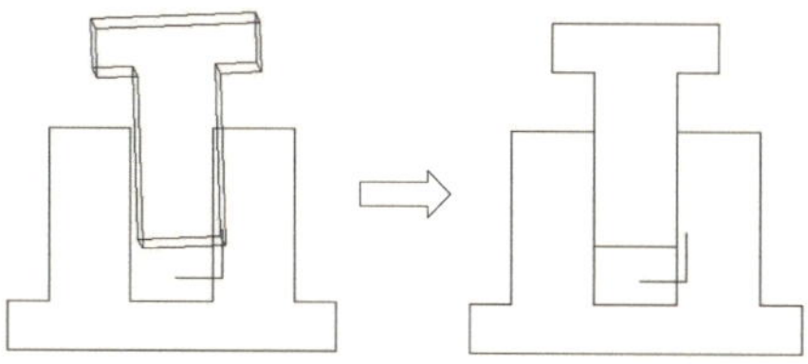

Fig. 8. Vision error correction by the non-linear methods. Left and right images show the result before and after the correction.

ambiguity mentioned in Section 2.1 and the calculation is implemented on the hardware. Using background subtraction and color detection, we only extract the target objects. By histogram of depths in each pixel, we roughly distinguish the moving and the fixed objects. We employ the method by Wheeler & Ikeuchi (1995) to extract the 6-DOF trajectory of the moving object. Figure 7 shows the results. And Figure 8 shows one example of the vision error correction by the non-linear method.

Figure 9 shows the result of applying the optimum vision error correction to the tracking result. The upper right and lower right graphs show the vision-error correction by the non-linear optimization (Takamatsu et al. (2007)) and the combination of the non-linear and linear optimization. Since translational displacement along the vertical direction is not constrained by any contacts, it is optimum that the displacement along the direction by the vision error correction is zero. In other words, the projected trajectories before and after the error correction should be the same. It is difficult to obtain the optimum error correction by using only the non-linear optimization, but it is possible to obtain it by combining the non-linear and linear methods. The lower left graph shows the trajectory projected on the xy-plane. The trajectory during the insertion is correctly adjusted as a straight line.

4. Estimating joint parameters

We often find the objects with several rigid parts which are connected by joints as shown in Fig. 10. These objects range from human body to daily-life artificial objects, such as door knobs and taps. Even in the constraint-free space, motion which seems to be virtually constrained by a joint can be seen. A constraint generated by a joint is useful for reducing vision errors. Even if the type of joint is known, the vision error correction involves estimation of joint parameters from a noise-contaminated observation. In this section, we describe the estimation of the

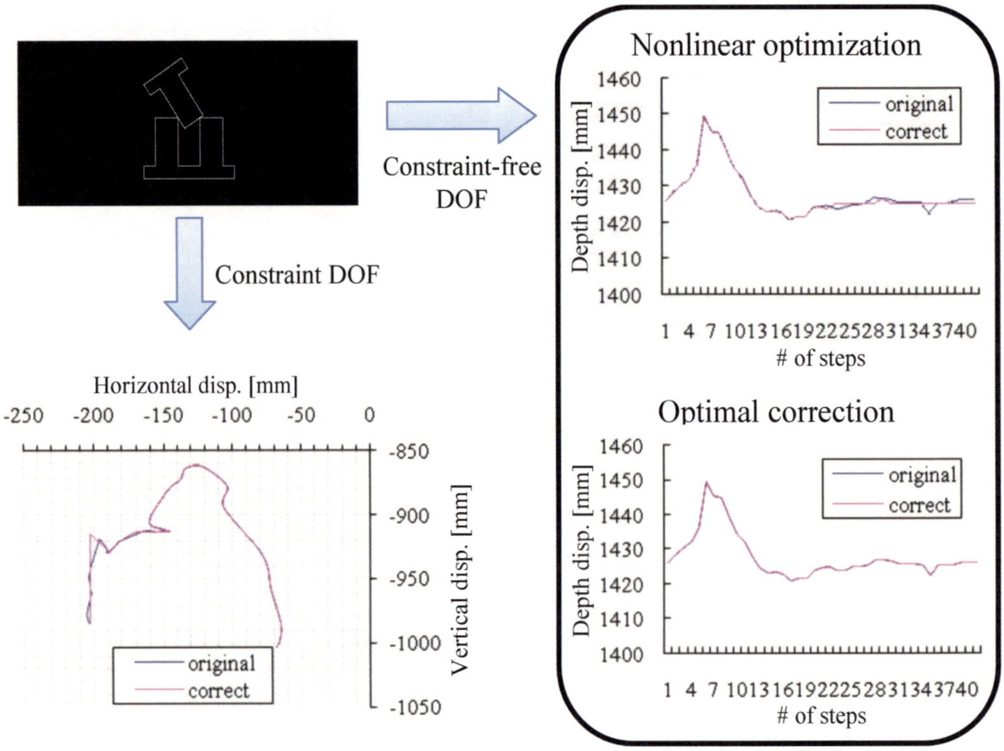

Fig. 9. Result of the vision error correction. The upper right and lower right graphs show the vision-error correction by the non-linear optimization (Takamatsu et al. (2007)), and combination of the non-linear and linear optimization. Displacement along the unconstrained direction is zero after the vision error correction (see the lower right graph), while trajectory during the insertion is correctly adjusted as the straight line (see the lower left graph).

revolute joint parameters as well as the vision error corrections. The estimation in the other types of joints is seen in Takamatsu (2004).

The trajectory of Link A with respect to coordinates of Link B, $({}^{B}\mathbf{t}_A(t), {}^{B}\Theta_A(t))$, is given as input, where the term ${}^{B}\mathbf{t}_A(t)$ $(\in \mathrm{R}^3)$ is the location and the term ${}^{B}\Theta_A(t)$ $(\in \mathrm{SO}(3))$ is the orientation at time t. As shown in Fig. 11, the joint parameters in the revolute joint are composed of the direction of revolute axis in coordinates of both Link A and Link B, ${}^{A}\mathbf{l}$, ${}^{B}\mathbf{l}$, and their location, ${}^{A}\mathbf{c}$, ${}^{B}\mathbf{c}$. Note that $|{}^{A}\mathbf{l}| = |{}^{B}\mathbf{l}| = 1$ holds. These terms must satisfy the following conditions:

$$ {}^{B}\mathbf{l} = {}^{B}\Theta_A(t)\, {}^{A}\mathbf{l}, \tag{10} $$

$$ {}^{B}\mathbf{c} = {}^{B}\Theta_A(t)\, {}^{A}\mathbf{c} + {}^{B}\mathbf{t}_A(t). \tag{11} $$

Considering the observation noise $\Delta\Theta(t)$ in orientation, Eq. (10) is reformulated as

$$ {}^{B}\mathbf{l} = \Delta\Theta(t)\, {}^{B}\Theta_A(t)\, {}^{A}\mathbf{l}. \tag{12} $$

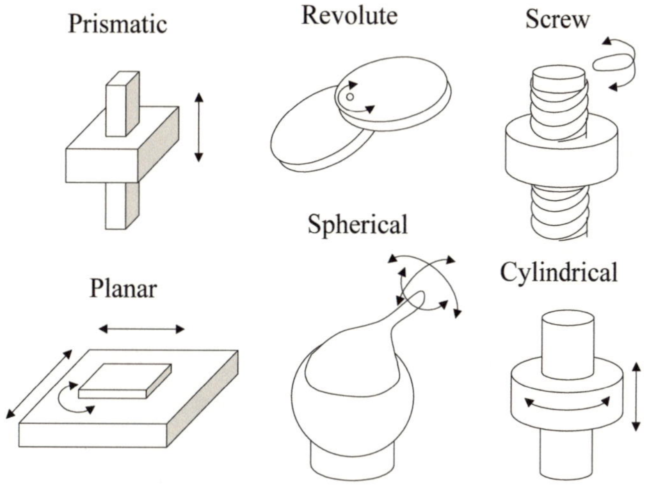

Fig. 10. Examples of joints

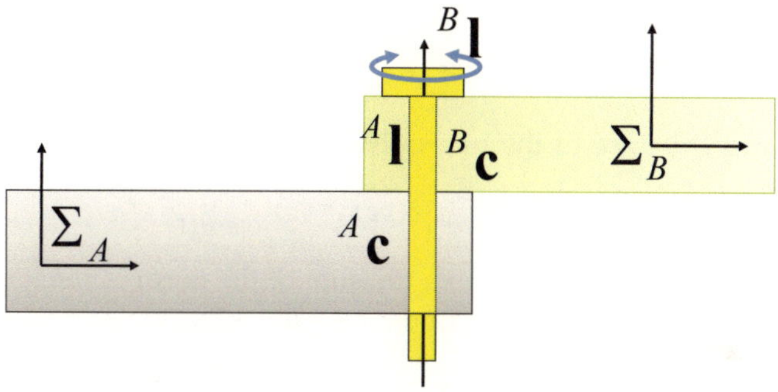

Fig. 11. Coordinates in revolute joint

We estimate the parameters in the least square manner, *i.e.*, estimate the parameters while minimizing the sum of the norm of $\Delta\Theta(t)$. The rotational displacement $\Delta\Theta$ is represented as a θ [deg] rotation about some axis $\mathbf{l}$, *i.e.*. $\Delta\Theta = \mathbf{R}(\mathbf{l}, \theta)$. Then, we define its norm as $1 - \cos\theta$. Note that θ is small enough, $1 - \cos\theta$ is approximated as $\frac{\theta^2}{2}$.
We decompose the noise term $\Delta\Theta(t)$ into a multiplication of two rotation matrices as shown in Eq. (13). One is a $\theta_1(t)$ [deg] rotation about the axis $^{B}\mathbf{l}$ and the other is a $\theta_2(t)$ [deg] rotation about the axis $\mathbf{l}(t)$, where $\forall t, {}^{B}\mathbf{l} \cdot \mathbf{l}(t) = 0$ holds.

$$\Delta\Theta(t) = \mathbf{R}({}^{B}\mathbf{l}, \theta_1(t))\mathbf{R}(\mathbf{l}(t)\theta_2(t)). \tag{13}$$

By substituting Eq. (13) into Eq. (12), Eq. (14) is obtained.

$$\mathbf{R}({}^{B}\mathbf{l}, \theta_1(t))\ {}^{B}\mathbf{l} = \mathbf{R}(\mathbf{l}(t), \theta_2(t))^{B}\Theta_A(t)\ {}^{A}\mathbf{l}. \tag{14}$$

The left part of this equation is constant for any $\theta_1(t)$, since $^{B}\mathbf{l}$ does not change after the rotation about the axis $^{B}\mathbf{l}$. Following the least square manner, we assume that $\theta_1(t) = 0$.

Thereafter, by multiplying the term ${}^{B}\mathbf{1}^{T}$ on the both sides from the right in Eq. (14), Eq. (15) is obtained. Note that we simply denote $\theta_2(t)$ as $\theta(t)$.

$$\mathbf{R}(-\mathbf{1}(t),\theta(t))^{B}\mathbf{1}\,{}^{B}\mathbf{1}^{T} = {}^{B}\Theta_{A}(t)\;{}^{A}\mathbf{1}\,{}^{B}\mathbf{1}^{T}. \tag{15}$$

The left side of Eq. (15) is written as follows:

$$(I - \sin\theta(t)[\mathbf{1}(t)]_{\times} + (1-\cos\theta(t))[\mathbf{1}(t)]_{\times}^{2})^{B}\mathbf{1}\,{}^{B}\mathbf{1}^{T},$$

where the matrix $[(x,y,z)]_{\times}$ is the skew symmetry matrix and is defined as

$$[(x,y,z)]_{\times} = \begin{pmatrix} 0 & -z & y \\ z & 0 & -x \\ -y & x & 0 \end{pmatrix}.$$

Through the actual calculation, it is proved that the following equations always hold:

$$\begin{aligned} \mathrm{Tr}({}^{B}\mathbf{1}\,{}^{B}\mathbf{1}^{T}) &= 1, \\ \mathrm{Tr}([\mathbf{1}(t)]_{\times}\,{}^{B}\mathbf{1}\,{}^{B}\mathbf{1}^{T}) &= 0, \\ \mathrm{Tr}([\mathbf{1}(t)]_{\times}^{2}\,{}^{B}\mathbf{1}\,{}^{B}\mathbf{1}^{T}) &= ({}^{B}\mathbf{1}\cdot\mathbf{1}(t))^{2} - 1 = -1, \end{aligned}$$

where $\mathrm{Tr}(\mathbf{M})$ returns the trace of the matrix $\mathbf{M}$. By using them, we obtain the following equation:

$$\mathrm{Tr}(\mathbf{R}(-\mathbf{1}(t),\theta(t))^{B}\mathbf{1}\,{}^{B}\mathbf{1}^{T}) = \cos\theta(t) \tag{16}$$

When the sum of $1-\cos\theta(t)$ is minimized, the sum of the norm of the noise term $\Delta\Theta(t)$ is minimized. We estimate the direction by minimizing the following equation.

$$({}^{A}\hat{\mathbf{1}},{}^{B}\hat{\mathbf{1}}) = \underset{{}^{A}\mathbf{1},{}^{B}\mathbf{1}}{\mathrm{argmin}} \sum_{t}(1 - \mathrm{Tr}({}^{B}\Theta_{A}(t)\;{}^{A}\mathbf{1}\,{}^{B}\mathbf{1}^{T})). \tag{17}$$

After estimating the direction, the orientation after the vision error correction ${}^{B}\hat{\Theta}_{A}(t)$ is obtained from the outer product of ${}^{B}\Theta_{A}(t)^{A}\mathbf{1}$ and ${}^{B}\mathbf{1}$. The displacement for the vision error correction corresponds to the matrix with minimum norm that matches the vector ${}^{B}\Theta_{A}(t)\;{}^{A}\mathbf{1}$ with the vector ${}^{B}\mathbf{1}$.

After estimating the corrected orientation, the location is estimated by the linear least square method, where $A(t) = \left(-{}^{B}\hat{\Theta}_{A}(t)\;I\right)$.

$$\left(\sum_{t} A(t)^{T}A(t)\right)\begin{pmatrix}{}^{A}\mathbf{c}\\{}^{B}\mathbf{c}\end{pmatrix} = \sum_{t} A(t)^{T}\,{}^{B}\mathbf{t}_{A}(t). \tag{18}$$

Since the matrix $\sum_{i} A(t)^{T}A(t)$ is not a full-rank matrix, the singular value decomposition is used to solve this equation.

Result We showed the estimation result from the observation using a real-time stereo vision system in Section 3. In this experiment, we used two LEGO parts, which are connected by the revolute joint. Figure 12 shows the tracking result.

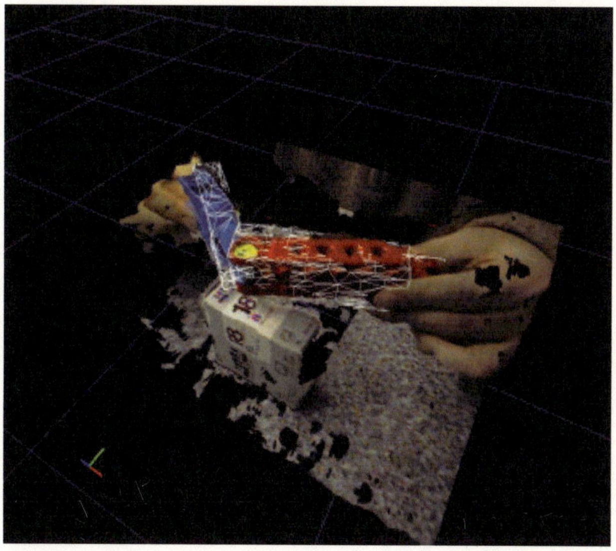

Fig. 12. Tracking result

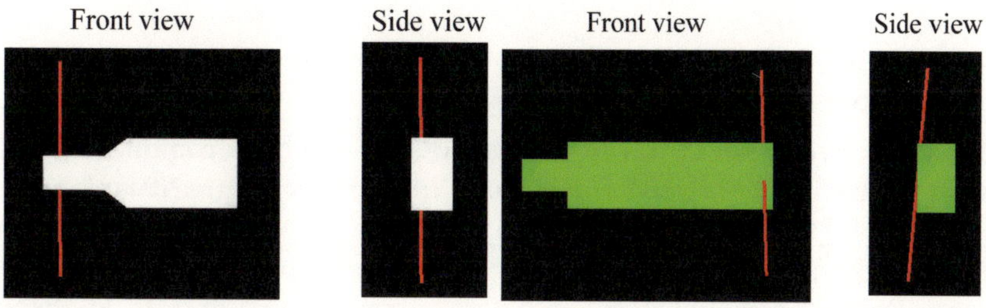

Fig. 13. Estimation result

Figure 13 shows the estimation result. The red line indicates the estimated revolute axis. The joint parameter of the blue LEGO block (corresponds to the white block in Fig. 13) is relatively accurate. If the noise distribution is accurately modeled, the maximum likelihood (ML) inference may improve the estimation. Unfortunately, it is difficult, perhaps impossible, to model the noise distribution. Outlier detection dissolves this poor estimation.

5. Modeling by implicit polynomial

To recognize the interaction of the objects, the differential properties of the object surface are often required. Generally, the differential operation amplifies the noise, and thus the object modeling method robust to the noise is highly demanded. Although we did not directly use the method mentioned in this section for the 3D data obtained from the stereo vision system, we would like to introduce modeling using an implicit polynomial which is very robust to noise.

Representation in implicit polynomial (IP) is advantageous in robustness against noise and occlusion, compactness of representation, and differentiability. And thus, many applications using IP's exist (*e.g.*Taubin & Cooper (1992)). Unlike the other parametric representations,

such as B-spline and NURBS, it is very easy to estimate the parameters of IP, given the target model.
IP with n-degree can be defined as follows:

$$\begin{aligned} f_n(\boldsymbol{x}) &= \sum_{0 \leq i,j,k; i+j+k \leq n} a_{ijk} x^i y^j z^k \\ &= \underbrace{(1\ x\ \ldots\ z^n)}_{\boldsymbol{m}(\boldsymbol{x})^T} \underbrace{(a_{000}\ a_{100}\ \cdots\ a_{00n})^T}_{\boldsymbol{a}}, \end{aligned} \quad (19)$$

where $\boldsymbol{x} = (x\ y\ z)$ represents coordinates in 3D space. In the IP representation, the object surface is modeled by a zero level set of the IP, *i.e.*, $\{\boldsymbol{x} | f_n(\boldsymbol{x}) = 0\}$. The IP's parameter corresponds to the coefficient $\boldsymbol{a}$. Given the target model in point cloud representation, such as $\{\boldsymbol{x}_i\}$, the parameters are estimated by the following steps:

1. manually assign the IP's degree.
2. solve the following simultaneous linear system, where M is the matrix whose i-th row corresponds to $\boldsymbol{m}(\boldsymbol{x}_i)$[5]:

$$M\boldsymbol{a} = \boldsymbol{b}. \quad (20)$$

3. Compare the modeling result to the target object. If it is not so accurate, change the degree and go back to Step 1.

Since it is not intuitive to select the appropriate degree n for the complicated shapes, this selection wastes time unnecessarily. Further, instability in higher degree IP is also problematic. We propose a method to adaptively select the appropriate degree by incrementally increasing the degree, while keeping the computational time. Incrementability of QR decomposition by the Gram-Schmidt orthogonalization plays a very important role in the proposed method (Zheng et al. (2010)). QR decomposition decomposes the given matrix M into two matrices Q, R as $M = QR$, where $Q^T Q = I$ holds and the matrix R is an upper triangle matrix. Since the Gram-Schmidt orthogonalization is conducted in an inductive manner, it offers the incrementability to the proposed method. To solve the coefficient $\boldsymbol{a}$ in each degree, we simply solve the upper triangle linear system, resulting in reducing the computational time. Eigenvalues provide information about stability in the calculation. Fortunately, eigenvalues of the upper triangle matrix are simply obtained by just checking the diagonal elements of the matrix.
We convert Eq. (20) to fit the QR decomposition. In the linear least square manner, the coefficient $\boldsymbol{a}$ should satisfy the following condition:

$$M^T M\boldsymbol{a} = M^T\boldsymbol{b}. \quad (21)$$

By substituting $M = QR$, the following equation is obtained:

$$R^T Q^T Q R\boldsymbol{a} = R^T Q^T \boldsymbol{b} \Rightarrow R\boldsymbol{a} = Q^T\boldsymbol{b} \stackrel{\text{def}}{=} \widetilde{\boldsymbol{b}}. \quad (22)$$

[5] Generally, the condition about the zero level set generates a constraint where $\boldsymbol{b} = \boldsymbol{0}$. Thus, the eigen method is used for the estimation (*e.g.*, Taubin (1991)). In order to increase calculation stability, other additional constraints are added (*e.g.*, M. Blane & Cooper (2000)), resulting in $\boldsymbol{b} \neq \boldsymbol{0}$. This can be solved using a simple linear solver.

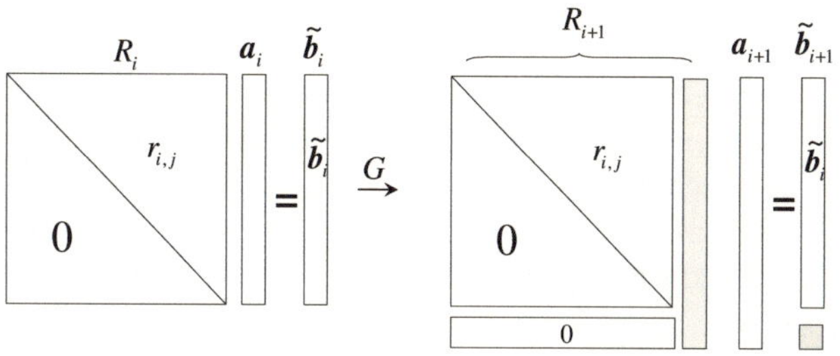

Fig. 14. Necessary calculation for going from the i-th step to the $i+1$-th step. Calculation results are reusable, except for the shaded part.

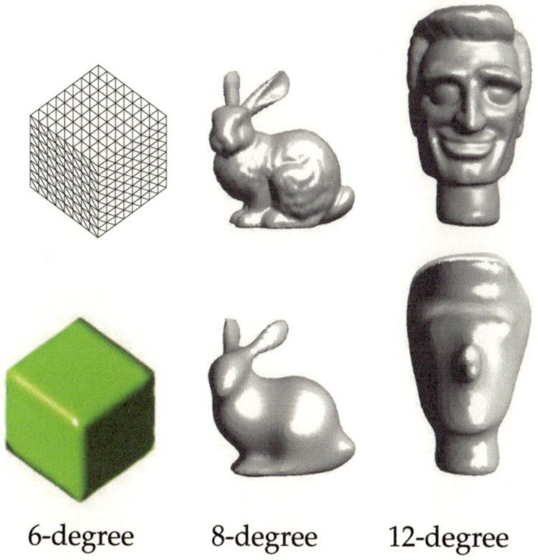

Fig. 15. Result of IP modeling. First row: original data. Second row: IP model.

As described above, QR decomposition is done by gradually applying the Gram-Schmidt orthogonalization to columns of the matrix M from left to right. When going from the i-th step to the $i+1$-th step, we only need to calculate the shaded part in Fig. 14; the other part is kept constant from the previous calculation. As a result, the calculation is totally accelerated. Regarding the numerical stability, we pay attention to the case where the conditional number of the matrix R becomes worse. The conditional number is usually defined as the ratio between the maximum and the minimum eigenvalues. Since the eigenvalues of the matrix R corresponds to the diagonal elements themselves, we simultaneously evaluate the numerical stability. If it tunes to be unstable, we ignore the corresponding column, which is added at this step, or partially apply the RR method (Sahin & Unel (2005); Tasdizen et al. (2000)). We increase the IP's degree until the modeling accuracy is sufficient.

Result Figure 15 shows the result of IP modeling. The cube consists of six planes so an IP with six degrees is appropriate. The paper (Zheng et al. (2010)) includes other IP modeling results. Since an IP models the shape considering global consistency, the model is useful for object recognition.

6. Conclusion

In this chapter, we described the vision error correction using various constraints, such as contact relation and mechanical joint. Further, we introduced the modeling method using an implicit polynomial which is very robust to noise. Stereo vision is simple, but potential technique to obtain 3D information. One disadvantage is the accuracy. We believe that vision error correction using prior knowledge becomes necessary research stream in real-world robot applications.

7. Acknowledgment

We would like to thank members of Ikeuchi laboratory (http://www.cvl.iis.u-tokyo.ac.jp) for providing the software, the experimental environment, and the fruitful comments. We would like to thank Mr. Garcia Ricardez Gustavo Alfonso for his useful feedback on this document.

8. References

Bay, H., Ess, A., Tuytelaars, T. & Gool, L. V. (2008). SURF: Speeded up robust features, *Comp. Vis. and Image Understanding* 110(3): 346–359.

Besl, P. J. & McKay, N. D. (1992). A method for registration of 3-d shapes, *IEEE Trans. on Patt. Anal. and Mach. Intell.* 14(2): 249–256.

Boykov, Y. & Kolmogorov, V. (2004). An experimental comparison of min-cut/max-flow algorithms for energy minimization in vision, *IEEE Trans. on Patt. Anal. and Mach. Intell.* 26(9): 1124–1137.

Brunton, A., Shu, C. & Roth, G. (2006). Belief propagation on the gpu for stereo vision, *Proc. of Canadian Conf. on Comp. and R. Vis.*

Chen, Y. & Medioni, G. (1991). Object modeling by registration of multiple range images, *Proc. of IEEE Int'l Conf. on R. and Auto. (ICRA).*

Felzenszwalb, P. & Huttenlocher, D. (2006). Efficient belief propagation for early vision, *Int'l J. of Comp. Vis.* 70: 41–54.

Fischler, M. A. & Bolles, R. C. (1981). Random sample consensus: A paradigm for model fitting with applications to image analysis and automated cartography, *Communications of the ACM* 24: 381–395.

Flusser, J. & Suk, T. (1994). A moment-based approach to registration of images with affine geometric distortion, *IEEE Trans. on Geoscience and Remote Sensing* 32(2): 382–387.

Hebert, M., Ikeuchi, K. & Delingette, H. (1995). A spherical representation for recognition of free-form surface, *IEEE Trans. on Patt. Anal. and Mach. Intell.* 17(7): 681–690.

Hirukawa, H. (1996). On motion planning of polyhedra in contact, *WAFR* .

Hirukawa, H., Matsui, T. & Takase, K. (1994). Automatic determination of possible velocity and applicable force of frictionless objects in contact from a geometric model, *IEEE Trans. on Robotics and Automation* 10(3): 309–322.

Huber, P. J. (1981). *Robust statistics*, Wiley-Interscience.

Ikeuchi, K. & Suehiro, T. (1994). Toward an assembly plan from observation part i: Task recognition with polyhedral objects, *IEEE Trans. on Robotics and Automation* 10(3): 368–385.

Ishikawa, H. (2009). Higher-order clique reduction in binary graph cut, *Proc. of Comp. Vis. and Patt. Recog. (CVPR).*

Johnson, A. E. & Hebert, M. (1999). Using spin images for efficient object recognition in cluttered 3d scenes, *IEEE Trans. on Patt. Anal. and Mach. Intell.* 21(5): 433–449.

Kang, S. B. & Ikeuchi, K. (1997). The complex egi: New representation for 3-d pose determination, *IEEE Trans. on Patt. Anal. and Mach. Intell.* 15(7): 707–721.

Kuniyoshi, Y., Inaba, M. & Inoue, H. (1994). Learning by watching: Extracting reusable task knowledge from visual observation of human performance, *IEEE Trans. on Robotics and Automation* 10(6): 799–822.

Lan, X., Roth, S., Huttenlocher, D. P. & Black, M. J. (2006). Efficient belief propagation with learned higher-order markov random fields, *Proc. of Euro. Conf. on Comp. Vis. (ICCV)*.

Lowe, D. (2004). Distinctive image features from scale-invariant key points, *Int'l J. of Comp. Vis.* 60(2): 91–110.

M. Blane, Z. L. & Cooper, D. (2000). The 3l algorithm for fitting implicit polynomial curves and surfaces to data, *IEEE Trans. on Patt. Anal. and Mach. Intell.* 22(3): 298–313.

Makadia, A., IV, A. P. & Daniilidis, K. (2006). Fully automatic registration of 3d point clouds, *Proc. of Comp. Vis. and Patt. Recog. (CVPR)*.

Ohwovoriole, M. S. & Roth, B. (1981). An extension of screw theory, *J. of Mechanical Design* 103: 725–735.

Potetz, B. (2007). Efficient belief propagation for vision using linear constraint nodes, *Proc. of Comp. Vis. and Patt. Recog. (CVPR)*.

Rusinkiewicz, S. & Levoy, M. (2001). Efficient variants of the icp algorithm, *Proc. of Int'l Conf. on 3-D Digital Imaging and Modeling*.

Sahin, T. & Unel, M. (2005). Fitting globally stabilized algebraic surfaces to range data, *Proc. of Int'l Conf. on Comp. Vis. (ICCV)*.

Scharstein, D. & Szeliski, R. (2002). A taxonomy and evaluation of dense two-frame stereo correspondence algorithm, *Int'l J. of Comp. Vis.* 47(1/2/3): 7–42.

Takamatsu, J. (2004). *Abstraction of Manipulation Tasks to Automatically Generate Robot Motion from Observation*, PhD thesis, the University of Tokyo.

Takamatsu, J., Kimura, H. & Ikeuchi, K. (2002). Calculating optimal trajectories from contact transitions, *Proc. of IEEE Int'l Conf. on Intell. R. and Sys. (IROS)*.

Takamatsu, J., Ogawara, K., Kimura, H. & Ikeuchi, K. (2007). Recognizing assembly tasks through human demonstration, *Int'l J. of Robotics Research* 26(7): 641–659.

Tasdizen, T., Tarel, J.-P. & Cooper, D. B. (2000). Improving the stability of algebraic curves for applications, *IEEE Trans. on Image Proc.* 9(3): 405–416.

Taubin, G. (1991). Estimation of planar curves, surfaces and nonplanar space curves defined by implicit equations with applications to edge and range image segmentation, *IEEE Trans. on Patt. Anal. and Mach. Intell.* 13(11): 1115–1138.

Taubin, G. & Cooper, D. (1992). *Symbolic and Numerical Computation for Artificial Intelligence*, Computational Mathematics and Applications, Academic Press, chapter 6.

Tsai, R. Y. (1986). An efficient and accurate camera calibration technique for 3d machine vision, *Proc. of Comp. Vis. and Patt. Recog. (CVPR)*.

Umeyama, S. (1991). Least-squares estimation of transformation parameters between two point patterns, *IEEE Trans. on Patt. Anal. and Mach. Intell.* 13(4).

Wheeler, M. D. & Ikeuchi, K. (1995). Sensor modeling, probabilistic hypothesis generation, and robust localization for object recognition, *IEEE Trans. on Patt. Anal. and Mach. Intell.* 17(3): 252–265.

Wolfson, H. J. & Rigoutsos, I. (1997). Geometric hashing: An overview, *Computing in Science and Engineering* 4(4): 10–21.

Zhang, Z. (2000). A flexible new technique for camera calibration, *IEEE Trans. on Patt. Anal. and Mach. Intell.* 22(11): 1330–1334.

Zheng, B., Takamatsu, J. & Ikeuchi, K. (2010). An adaptive and stable method for fitting implicit polynomial curves and surfaces, *IEEE Trans. on Patt. Anal. and Mach. Intell.* 32(3): 561–568.